Beginning ENGLISH DAY BY DAY

MICHAEL RODDY

Academic Therapy Publications
Novato, California

Cover Design: Jill Zwicky

 For information address Academic Therapy Publications, 20 Commercial Blvd., Novato, CA 94949-6191.

International Standard Book Number: 0-87879-907-9

7 6 5 4 3 2 1 0 9 8
5 4 3 2 1 0 9 8 7 6

Contents

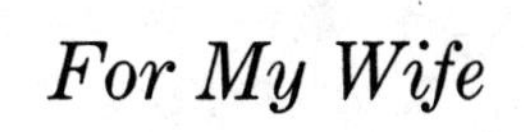
For My Wife

To the Teacher

Beginning English Day by Day aims to meet the needs of students who are beginning to learn English and help them reach any goals they might have: to advance vocational education; to get a job or find a better one; to go on to higher education; or simply to meet the demands of everyday living in our country.

This book stresses the basic language skills of grammar, reading, writing, and pronunciation in the context of life situations where competency in conversational and written skills and in problem-solving techniques can be critical. Included in the content are exercises in basic and higher thinking skills. The format of the twelve units is sequential.

Recent research on learning styles and different kinds of intelligences has indicated that ESL texts with their auditory/oral emphasis cover only one aspect of learning and knowledge. When using this book, teachers should also consider visual and kinesthetic learning styles, inductive and deductive processing, field sensitivity and field independence, and, especially, self-directed learning. Students come to the classroom with a wealth of experience to tap; this book serves as a basic tool which can do just that. Each unit should be supported by objects and ideas from the students' real lives. In a word, it is strongly suggested that the teacher connect the students from the written word to the real world. Let them experience how language reflects life.

I. Vocabulary

In order to prepare the student for more effective participation in the activities of the unit, lists of key words relating to the unit's theme are introduced and separated into applicable subject areas. Teachers are encouraged to bring in as much realia, visuals or actual objects as possible that relate to these key words. Students may be encouraged to look up the words in their own language dictionaries when necessary. The teacher should pronounce each word and give the students the opportunity to explain it. This helps to establish just how much the students already know and where their experience lies in the subject area. For example, a student who is a nurse can help enormously with the health unit by adding insight and relevance to the meanings of these words. Brainstorming is also often helpful in explaining the vocabulary words. The main idea in this section of each unit is to establish the theme and to set the tone for what is to follow.

II. Conversation

Three conversations using the unit theme and related vocabulary are presented. Some of the conversations have structured exercises that give students opportunities to practice in pairs.

III. Reading

The reading selections for each unit concern the unit's theme and how the lives of various adults fit into it. Exercises follow with questions to answer. At the beginning the exercises require only fill-in answers; they gradually work up to full questions to answer and then call for some answers that demand inductive or deductive reasoning.

IV. Structure

This section introduces basic grammar. The material is presented sequentially, and all of the examples and practice exercises clearly pertain to each unit's theme. Grammar, again, is not the total goal of this book. Competence in communication skills is an equally important objective.

V. Writing

These exercises are controlled in the first part of the book but gradually orient the student to writing on his own. First, the words must be put in correct order in a sentence and then copied in the form of a paragraph. Gradually the students are asked to write paragraphs about their own experiences in that subject area.

VI. Pronunciation

The pronunciation section consists of practice drills of vowels, probably the most troublesome area for beginning ESL students. Students can repeat the words after the teacher and then say them aloud on their own. There is a short exercise in which the teacher can pronounce some of the words (or new ones with the same sound) and have students write them.

VII. Life Skills

This section presents practical examples of life skills that have been mentioned throughout the unit. This is where language and reality meet. Students are asked to answer questions involving real life situational use of English.

VIII. Critical Thinking

With the increasing awareness and concern for critical thinking in education, this section of the unit represents one of the true basics of tomorrow. More and more the real world is demanding people who can creatively and skillfully think for themselves. The two photographs in this unit and the accompanying vocabulary words, phrases, and sentences facilitate a beginning student's approach to critical thinking. The student needs only to place below the photograph the appropriate words that relate to or identify it. There is opportunity here for teachers to go beyond the regular exercise through discussion on related issues the students may wish to bring up. Often ideas that have several meanings can stimulate a student to speak more expressively than he thinks he can, or give the student the opportunity to practice the information learned throughout the unit. In small groups he has the opportunity to put together his conversational, problem-solving, and cooperative learning skills.

■ ■ ■ ■ ■

This text requires interaction between teacher and student and among class members. This is an active, involved instructional approach. (Teacher can consult answer key for explanation of tasks.)

There is a deliberate attempt to integrate all aspects of language into a useful tool for everyday living in an English-speaking culture. It is the author's intent that the student will not only learn from and enjoy the learning experience but will also feel challenged, in a very active sense, to apply all of the methods, exercises, and vocabulary to his own life.

NOTE: At the end of the book there is an addendum which provides the instructor and student with extra information such as the cursive alphabet, irregular verbs, and measurements that can be applied to the various units throughout the book.

INTRODUCTION

Objectives

Competencies:
Recognizing Letters, Words, and Numbers

Structure
Alphabet
Cardinal Numbers 1-10

Alphabet

A a	B b	C c	D d	E e	F f	G g
H h	I i	J j	K k	L l	M m	N n
O o	P p	Q q	R r	S s	T t	U u
V v	W w	X x	Y y	Z z		

Write

_______ _______ _______ _______ _______ _______ _______

_______ _______ _______ _______ _______ _______ _______

_______ _______ _______ _______ _______ _______ _______

_______ _______ _______ _______ _______

____

NO PARKING

____
____

OPEN

____

CLOSED

____

HOSPITAL

____

WOMEN

____

DANGER

____

RESTAURANT

____

EMPLOYEES ONLY

____
____

FOR SALE

____
____

MEN

____

Look 

1. A	z	i	a	n	14. Q	b	p	d	q
2. N	n	m	u	w	15. Z	s	z	e	a
3. J	g	y	i	j	16. T	h	t	k	l
4. B	b	p	d	y	17. C	e	a	c	r
5. E	f	a	e	c	18. F	f	l	w	p
6. X	v	z	h	x	19. W	v	u	w	f
7. U	w	u	v	t	20. Y	d	y	i	c
8. H	k	n	h	s	21. G	y	h	j	g
9. P	p	q	d	y	22. S	s	a	e	o
10. R	r	l	c	z	23. V	u	w	i	v
11. D	o	w	p	d	24. O	t	s	o	a
12. L	f	h	l	b	25. M	m	n	w	u
13. K	k	b	a	l	26. I	e	i	o	v

Listen

1.	t	d	p	14.	T	L	K
2.	f	h	t	15.	f	t	l
3.	H	T	X	16.	e	o	c
4.	a	e	o	17.	I	T	L
5.	z	y	j	18.	n	r	m
6.	U	V	W	19.	u	n	v
7.	p	b	d	20.	O	C	A
8.	y	j	g	21.	j	y	g
9.	N	U	O	22.	E	A	C
10.	z	s	g	23.	b	d	p
11.	j	y	g	24.	K	H	W
12.	v	u	i	25.	p	q	d
13.	A	E	R	26.	v	x	q

Listen

1. n a ___ e
2. R o ___ e r t
3. c ___ t y
4. ___ d d ___ e s s
5. M r. C a r ___ o n
6. t ___ l e ___ ___ o n e

(continued)

7. Mar___ Br___w___
8. ___irs___
9. ___ast
10. ___o___ntry
11. a___e
12. ___ail
13. Mrs. Da___i___son
14. ___al___
15. ___ip
16. bo___
17. ___uick

Look

LAST	BIRTHPLACE	LANGUAGE	NATIONALITY
NAME	DATE OF BIRTH	MALE	ADDRESS
FIRST	COUNTRY	FEMALE	TELEPHONE
AGE	ZIP CODE	YOU	

Example:

(L A S T) I E C O U N T R Y G H
D G V X W G M I G A F I R S T
Y E Y O U K T W Q M W P U I D
A N F B N S C Z M E Y I L B L
D A T E O F B I R T H N C T A
Z G Z S W T U V R I N C F X N
I N A T I O N A L I T Y E A G
P S P B X N T O R F G L M T U
C S V N S J D M A L E F A E A
O B I R T H P L A C E N L Y G
D A D D R E S S C V R I E E E
E F E M A T E L E P H O N E B

Numbers

1 one	2 two	3 three	4 four	5 five
6 six	7 seven	8 eight	9 nine	10 ten

Listen

_________ _________ _________ _________ _________

_________ _________ _________ _________ _________

Telephone

Emergency: 911

Bert Boone: 555-6832

Police:________________

You:________________ Area Code:________________

Address	**Street**	**City**	**Zip Code**
Sue Young	841 Maple Street	Millbrae	94010
School	__________	________	________
You	__________	________	________

Apartment Number

Sam Johnson	5
__________	____

UNIT 1

IDENTIFICATION

"Hello, what's your name?"
"My name is Steve."
"Where are you from?"
"I'm from China."

Objectives

Competencies:
Cardinal Numbers 11-20
Greetings and Salutations
Identification
Completing Forms

Structure:
Verb: To Be
Subject Pronouns: I, You, He, She, It, We, They
Nouns: Singular and Plural

Pronunciation:
short a (ă)

I. Vocabulary

1. name
2. first
3. last
4. address
5. street
6. city
7. state
8. zip code
9. country
10. birthplace
11. age
12. nationality
13. school
14. student
15. teacher
16. telephone number
17. Please Print
18. language
19. spell
20. sure
21. what
22. you
23. where
24. here
25. How are you?
26. fine
27. live
28. until tomorrow

Country	**—**	**Nationality**
Mexico	—	Mexican
Germany	—	German
Brazil	—	Brazilian
Russia	—	Russian
Iran	—	Iranian
Italy	—	Italian
Japan	—	Japanese
China	—	Chinese
Vietnam	—	Vietnamese
Poland	—	Polish
Sweden	—	Swedish
Spain	—	Spanish
______________	—	______________
______________	—	______________
______________	—	______________
______________	—	______________
______________	—	______________

My native country is ______________________ .

My nationality is ______________________ .

Numbers 11-20

11	=	eleven	16	=	sixteen
12	=	twelve	17	=	seventeen
13	=	thirteen	18	=	eighteen
14	=	fourteen	19	=	nineteen
15	=	fifteen	20	=	twenty

Listen:

________ ________ ________ ________ ________

________ ________ ________ ________ ________

II. Conversation

A.

James: Hello, my name is James.
Lisa: Hi, I'm Lisa. Nice to meet you.
James: Nice meeting you, too.
Lisa: Where are you from?
James: I'm from Lebanon. I'm Lebanese.
Lisa: I'm from Bolivia. I'm Bolivian.

B.

Bob: Hello. How are you?
Mary: I am fine. And you?
Bob: Not bad. How is your mother?
Mary: Very good, thank you.
Bob: Bye.
Mary: OK, see you later.
Bob: Sure, until tomorrow.

C.

Tom: Hello, what's your name?
Jane: It's Jane Burns.
Tom: How do you spell that?
Jane: J—A—N—E B—U—R—N—S.
Tom: Thanks. My last name is Johnson.
Jane: What street do you live on?
Tom: On Elm Street.
Jane: Excuse me?
Tom: E—L—M.
Jane: Oh, Elm Street. That's near here.

III. Reading

David Brett is a student. His native country is France. His nationality is French. He lives in Middletown. His address is 465 Delaware Street. He lives in an apartment. His apartment number is 5. His telephone number is 555-9821. His mother and father live in Paris, France.

Exercise R-1:

1. David Brett is a ____________________ .
2. ____________________ is his last name.
3. ____________________ is his first name.

4. His ______________________ is France.
5. His nationality is ______________________ .
6. He lives in ______________________ .
7. His ______________________ is 465 Delaware Street.
8. He lives in an ______________________ .
9. His ______________________ is number five.
10. His phone number is ______________________ .
11. His parents live in ______________________ .

IV. Structure

A. Verb: To Be and Subject Pronouns

(I, You, He, She, It, We, They)

Subject Pronoun Singular	Verb To Be	Subject Pronoun Plural	Verb To Be
I	am	We	are
You	are	You	are
He	is	They	are
She	is		
It	is		

Exercise S-1:

Example: He is a student.

1. I ______________ a student.
2. They ______________ from Mexico.
3. He ______________ Chinese.
4. We ______________ students.
5. You ______________ from Japan.
6. It ______________ a registration form.
7. She ______________ Polish.
8. They ______________ Brazilian.
9. He ______________ a teacher.
10. It ______________ a state.

Exercise S-2:

Example: Tomas is from Mexico.
a. He   b. We   c. They

1. Bob is in Los Angeles.
   a. They   b. He   c. I
2. The students are here.
   a. They   b. She   c. It
3. Mary is from Switzerland.
   a. You   b. We   c. She
4. Bill and I are from Panama.
   a. He   b. We   c. I
5. The form is here.
   a. I   b. They   c. It
6. You and Susan are students.
   a. You   b. He   c. She

Exercise S-3:

Example: Chicago is a city.

1. California ______________ a state.
2. Mary ______________ from Canada.
3. John and Sam ______________ students.
4. San Francisco ______________ a city.
5. Susan and Kim ______________ here.

B. Contractions

I am = I'm	He is = He's	They are = They're
You are = You're	She is = She's	
We are = We're	It is = It's	

I am a student. = I'm a student.
They are nice people. = They're nice people.
He is from South America. = He's from South America.
We are in the United States. = We're in the United States.
She is from Iran. = She's from Iran.
It is a form. = It's a form.
You are a student. = You're a student.

Exercise S-4:

Example: theyre <u>they're</u>

1. hes ____________
2. Im ____________
3. its ____________
4. theyre ____________
5. shes ____________
6. youre ____________
7. were ____________

C. **Nouns (Singular and Plural)**

Exercise S-5:

Example: One form Two forms

One book	Two ____________
One pencil	Two ____________
One pen	Five ____________
One state	Six ____________
One language	Nine ____________
One notebook	Seven ____________
One ____________	Four erasers
One ____________	Eight names
One ____________	Ten numbers

Exercise S-6:

1. The students ____________ (is/are) in the class.
2. The city ____________ (is/are) in the state.
3. The pencils ____________ (is/are) here.
4. The book ____________ (is/are) there.
5. The teacher ____________ (is/are) in the class.

V. Writing

Exercise W-1:

Example: am student I a   I am a student.

students are They ______________________.

come You Italy from ______________________.

form a is registration It ______________________.

is Japanese He ______________________.

people nice We're ______________________.

VI. Pronunciation

Short a (ă)

last	nationality	address	at
bag	taxi cab	man	lamp
flat	pan	can	bath
back	hat	tack	

1. ______________   6. ______________
2. ______________   7. ______________
3. ______________   8. ______________
4. ______________   9. ______________
5. ______________   10. ______________

VII. Life Skills

Form A

CALIFORNIA
DRIVER LICENSE

J7891650
James J. Cool
747 Elm St.
San Mateo, CA 94401

X James J. Cool

Form B

Credit Union   MEMBER I.D.

NAME MARY HART

ADDRESS 1516 CYPRESS AVE.
BURLINGAME, CA 94010

PHONE (415) 375-4797

A. Form—Driver's License

Exercise L-1:

1. What is his first name?

   ____

2. What is his last name?

   ____

3. What is his address?

   ____

4. What is his license number?

   ____

B. Form—Credit Union

Exercise L-2:

1. What is her first name?

   ____

2. What is her last name?

   ____

3. What is her address?

   ____

4. What is her zip code?

   ____

5. What is her phone number?

   ____

C. Registration Form

DATE ______________________ MALE_____ FEMALE_____

NAME ____
LAST FIRST

____
ADDRESS CITY STATE ZIP CODE

________________ ________________ ________________
DATE OF BIRTH BIRTHPLACE NATIONALITY

VIII. Critical Thinking

A.

B.

Vocabulary

man	work	class	job
office	book	woman	study
school	answer phone		

He is a student.
She is at work.
He is in class.
She is a worker.

A.	B.
1. ____________	1. ____________
2. ____________	2. ____________
3. ____________	3. ____________
4. ____________	4. ____________
5. ____________	5. ____________
6. ____________	6. ____________
7. ____________	7. ____________

UNIT 2

TIME

What time is it? When is my appointment? Time is important in our lives. This unit is all about time in our lives.

Objectives

Competencies:

Cardinal Numbers 21-100
Days of the Week
Making an Appointment
Telling Time (1)
The Weather

Structure

Irregular Nouns, Singular and Plural
Demonstrative Pronouns: This, That, These, Those
Verb *To Be*, Negative and Question
Contractions
Questions: What, Who, When, What Time

Pronunciation:

long a (ā)

I. Vocabulary

A. Time

1. clock
2. hour
3. late
4. early
5. date
6. break
7. closed
8. open
9. What time?
10. When?

B. Unit Vocabulary

1. breakfast
2. lunch
3. dinner
4. favorite
5. bad
6. good
7. factory
8. from
9. like
10. desk
11. pen
12. pencil
13. doctor (Dr.)
14. How about you?
15. Who?
16. What?

C. Weather

Sunny	Raining	Windy	Stormy	Cloudy	Snowing	Foggy

Temperature

Degree = °
Fahrenheit = F
Centigrade = C

32 F/0 C	50 F/10 C	70 F/21 C	100 F/38 C
Cold	Cool	Warm	Hot

Exercise V-1:

Example: The temperature is 32 degrees F. It is cold.

1. The temperature is 38 degrees C. It is ____________________.
2. The temperature is 50 degrees F. It is ____________________.
3. The temperature is 21 degrees C. It is ____________________.
4. The temperature is 0 degrees C. It is ____________________.
5. The temperature is 70 degrees F. It is ____________________.

Today the temperature is ____________ degrees. It is ____________.

D. Numbers 21-100

21	twenty-one	27	twenty-seven	60	sixty
22	twenty-two	28	twenty-eight	70	seventy
23	twenty-three	29	twenty-nine	80	eighty
24	twenty-four	30	thirty	90	ninety
25	twenty-five	40	forty	100	one hundred
26	twenty-six	50	fifty		

Exercise V-2:

Example: 25 twenty-five

1. 38 ____________________
2. 43 ____________________
3. 84 ____________________
4. 52 ____________________

(continued)

5. 95 ____________ 8. 31 ____________

6. 67 ____________ 9. 76 ____________

7. 99 ____________ 10. 44 ____________

Exercise V-3:

Example: twenty-three <u>23</u>

1. ninety-six ________ 6. eighty-four ________

2. seventy-seven ________ 7. thirty-three ________

3. fifty-one ________ 8. ninety-two ________

4. forty-eight ________ 9. thirty-nine ________

5. sixty-two ________ 10. sixty-six ________

Exercise V-4:

Listen

1. ____ 4. ____ 7. ________ 10. ________

2. ____ 5. ____ 8. ________ 11. ________

3. ____ 6. ____ 9. ________ 12. ________

E. Days of the Week

Sunday/S/Sun Monday/M/Mon Tuesday/T/Tues
Wednesday/W/Wed Thursday/Th/Thur Friday/F/Fri
Saturday/S/Sat

Today is ________________.

Exercise V-5:

Listen

________ ________ ________ ________

________ ________ ________

F. Time (1)

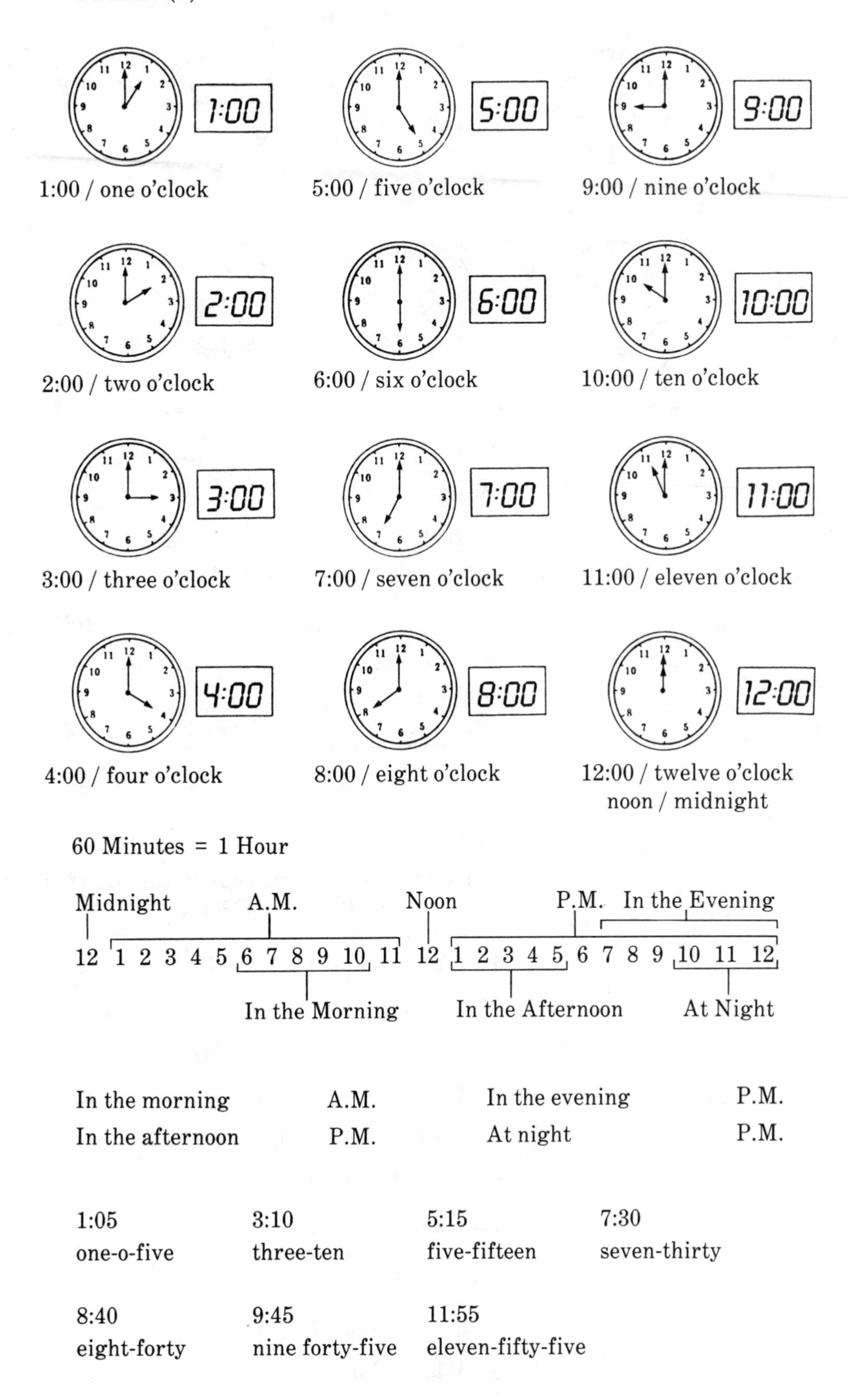

1:00 / one o'clock

5:00 / five o'clock

9:00 / nine o'clock

2:00 / two o'clock

6:00 / six o'clock

10:00 / ten o'clock

3:00 / three o'clock

7:00 / seven o'clock

11:00 / eleven o'clock

4:00 / four o'clock

8:00 / eight o'clock

12:00 / twelve o'clock
noon / midnight

60 Minutes = 1 Hour

In the morning	A.M.	In the evening	P.M.
In the afternoon	P.M.	At night	P.M.

1:05	3:10	5:15	7:30
one-o-five	three-ten	five-fifteen	seven-thirty
8:40	9:45	11:55	
eight-forty	nine forty-five	eleven-fifty-five	

Exercise V-6:

What time is it?

1. ____________ 2. ____________ 3. ____________ 4. ____________ 5. ____________

6. ____________ 7. ____________ 8. ____________ 9. ____________ 10. ____________

Exercise V-7:

What time is it?

Examples: 4:00 It's four o'clock.
6:15 It's six-fifteen.

1. 3:00 ____________
2. 2:00 ____________
3. 8:10 ____________
4. 12:05 ____________
5. 4:00 ____________
6. 10:30 ____________
7. 9:00 ____________
8. 11:45 ____________
9. 1:20 ____________
10. 7:35 ____________

Exercise V-8:

Examples: It's 3 o'clock in the afternoon. It's 3 P.M.
It's 11 A.M. It's 11 o'clock in the morning.

1. It's 6:15 in the morning. It's ____________.
2. It's 4 P.M. It's 4 o'clock ____________.
3. It's 6:00 P.M. It's 6 o'clock ____________.
4. It's 7:30 in the evening. It's ____________.
5. It's 10 o'clock at night. It's ____________.
6. It's 9:20 A.M. It's 9:20 ____________.
7. It's from 8 A.M. to 4 P.M. It's ____________.

Exercise V-9:

1. When is breakfast? It is at ____________ o'clock.
2. When is lunch? ____________.

3. When is dinner? ______________________.

4. When is school? It is from ______________ to ______________.

5. When is work? It is from ______________ to ______________.

II. Conversation

A.

Carl: What time is it?
Ed: It's 10:30.
Carl: Oh no, I'm late for work.
Ed: That's too bad.
Carl: Wait a minute. What's today?
Ed: It's Tuesday.
Carl: Oh good. My job is from Wednesday to Sunday.

B.

Sandra: How's the weather today?
Tim: It's cloudy and cold.
Sandra: In my native country it's hot.
Tim: I like warm weather. How about you?
Sandra: I like the rain.

C.

1	2	3	4
a) morning	nine	Friday	Thursday
b) afternoon	three	Tuesday	Monday
c) evening	seven	Wednesday	Tuesday

Bob: Hi. How are you this ______________ ?
(1)

Kay: Fine. And how are you?
Bob: Not too bad.
Kay: What time is it?
Bob: It's ______________ o'clock.
(2)

Kay: Oh, I'm late.
Bob: For what?
Kay: For my appointment on ______________ .
(3)

Bob: But today is ______________ .
(4)

Kay: Oh good.

III. Reading

Antonio is from Mexico. He is a factory worker. His job is from Monday to Friday, from 8 in the morning to 5 in the afternoon. His breakfast is at home at 8 A.M. His lunch is at the factory from 12:30 to 1:00 P.M. His breaks are from 10 to 10:15 in the morning and from 2 to 2:15 in the afternoon. His dinner is at home at 6 o'clock. His English class is from 7 to 9 in the evening. At 10 o'clock he is very tired.

Exercise R-1:

1. Antonio is from ____________________ .
2. He is a ____________________ worker.
3. His job is Monday, ____________________ , Wednesday, ____________________ , and ____________________ .
4. The hours of his job are from __________ to __________ .
5. His breakfast is at ____________________ at 7 o'clock.
6. His lunch is from __________ to __________ .
7. His ____________________ are fifteen minutes.
8. His dinner is at home at ____________________ .
9. His English class is ____________________ hours.
10. He is ____________________ at 10 o'clock.

IV. Structure

A. Irregular Nouns, Singular and Plural

	S	P
s, sh, ch add *es*	dress	dress<u>es</u>
	dish	dish<u>es</u>
	watch	watch<u>es</u>
y add *ies*	lady	lad<u>ies</u>
	baby	bab<u>ies</u>

S	P
woman	women
man	men
child	children
life	lives
foot	feet
tooth	teeth

Exercise S-1:

Example: (library) The libraries are in the city.

1. (city) The ______________________ are beautiful.
2. (country) The ______________________ are interesting.
3. (glass) The ______________________ are pretty.
4. (family) The ______________________ are here.
5. (child) The ______________________ are at school.
6. (boss) The ______________________ are at work.
7. (class) The ______________________ are interesting.
8. (woman) The ______________________ are factory workers.
9. (match) The ______________________ are here.
10. (brush) The ______________________ are new.
11. (man) The ______________________ are students.
12. (secretary) The ______________________ work from 9 to 5.
13. (university) The ______________________ are in the state.
14. (life) The ______________________ of students are interesting.

B. Demonstrative Pronouns: This, That, These, Those

What is this?	This is a knife.	It's a knife.
What are these?	These are knives.	They're knives.
What is that?	That is a peach.	It's a peach.
What are those?	Those are peaches.	They're peaches.

Exercise S-2:

Student 1	Student 2
What is this?	This is a pen.
What is that?	That is a desk.
What are these?	These are pens.
What are those?	Those are desks.
What is this?	______________________ .
______________________ ?	That is a ______________ .
______________________ ?	These are ______________ .
What are those?	______________________ .

C. Verb: To Be, Negative and Question

I am not	Am I?
You are not	Are you?
He is not	Is he?
She is not	Is she?
It is not	Is it?
We are not	Are we?
They are not	Are they?

D. Contractions

I am not = I'm not	You are not = You aren't
He is not = He isn't	She is not = She isn't
It is not = It isn't	We are not = We aren't
They are not = They aren't	

Exercise S-3:

Example: Is she a student? No, she isn't.

1. _______ they students? No, they _______________ .
2. _______ Nicole from Poland? No, she _______________ .
3. _______ Marco Brazilian? No, he _______________ .
4. _______ we late? No, we _______________ .
5. _______ it early? No, it _______________ .
6. _______ you a factory worker? No, I _______________ .
7. _______ I late? No, you _______________ .
8. _______ you tired? No, I _______________ .
9. _______ Steven from China? No, _______________ .
10. _______ Mary and Karen students? No, _______________ .

Is Mr. Lee here? No, he isn't.
Are the teachers at school? Yes, they are.

_______________________ ? No, _______________________ .
_______________________ ? No, _______________________ .
_______________________ ? Yes, _______________________ .
_______________________ ? Yes, _______________________ .

E. Questions: What, Who, When, What Time, What Day

What is this? It's a pen.
Who is this? It's Carl.
When is this? It's on Wednesday at one o'clock.
What time is this? It's at two o'clock.
What day is it? It's Thursday.

Exercise S-4:

Example: Who is this? It's Miyuki.

1. ____________ is that? That's a book.
2. ____________ are they? They're students.
3. ____________ is the program? It's on Friday at 7 o'clock.
4. ____________ are those? They are dictionaries.
5. ____________ is that? It's the teacher.
6. ____________ is the movie? It's at 4 o'clock.
7. ____________ is your name? My name is Gabriel.
8. ____________ is the appointment? It's on Thursday.

Who ____________________? ____________________.
What ____________________? ____________________.
When ____________________? ____________________.
What time ____________________? ____________________.
What day ____________________? ____________________.

F. How Old Are You?

How old is Bob? Bob is 22 years old.
How old is Elizabeth? Elizabeth is 35 years old.
How old are you? I am ____________ years old.

V. Writing

are Who people those? ______________________________
factory are They workers ______________________________
is 8 A.M. from Work 4 P.M. to ______________________________
noon Lunch at is ______________________________
They at are 5 tired o'clock ______________________________
7 Dinner at o'clock is ______________________________

Copy

____

____

____

____

____

____

VI. Pronunciation

long a (ā)

plane	date	nail
plate	rain	cake
train	late	face
day	May	April
eight	baby	native
conversation	favorite	ladies

Listen

1. ________ 2. ________ 3. ________ 4. ________

5. ________ 6. ________ 7. ________ 8. ________

VII. Life Skills

A. Appointment

Dr. Stain Wednesday 9 A.M.	Dr. Rail Thursday 1 P.M.	Dr. Pane Monday 3:30 P.M.	Dr. Clay Friday 10:45 A.M.

Exercise L-1:

1. When is the appointment with Dr. Rail?

   ____

2. What day is the appointment with Dr. Stain?

   ____

3. What time is the appointment with Dr. Pane?

   ____

4. Who is the doctor for the appointment on Monday at 3:30 P.M.?

____

5. Is the appointment with Dr. Stain in the morning?

____

6. Is the appointment with Dr. Clay in the afternoon?

____

7. Is the appointment with Dr. Rail in the morning or afternoon?

____

B. Time

1.
MOVIE
"RAMBO AND PEACE"
Tonight 7 and 9:30

2.
BUS STOP
5 P.M.
7 P.M.
9 P.M.

3.
TV PROGRAMS

6 P.M.	News
7 P.M.	"Racism"
8 P.M.	Music

4.
MUSEUM
Open: Tuesdays—Saturdays
10 A.M.—5 P.M.
Sunday 1 P.M.—5 P.M.

5.
NO PARKING
Thursday 6 - 9 A.M.

6.
MARY'S STORE
Back At

Exercise L-2:

1. What time is the movie "Rambo and Peace"?
   ____
2. What time is the TV program "Racism"?
   ____
3. Is the museum open on Monday?
   ____
4. Is the bus here at 7 in the evening?
   ____
5. Is parking OK on Wednesdays?
   ____
6. When is the TV news?
   ____
7. What time is the museum open on Sunday?
   ____
8. When is Mary's store open?
   ____
9. Is parking OK on Thursday at 8 in the morning?
   ____

C. Weather

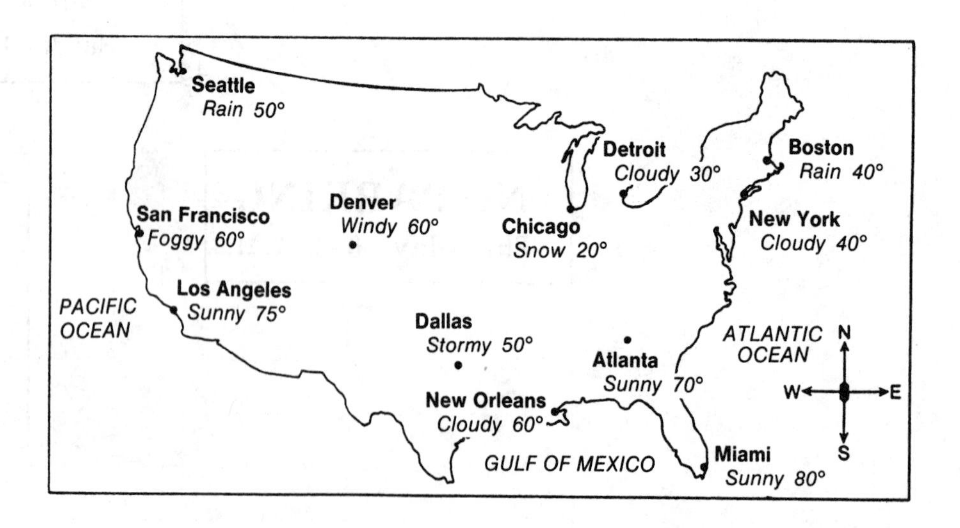

Exercise L-3:

Example: What's the weather in Chicago? It's snowing.

1. What's the weather in New York? ____________
2. Is it raining in Boston? ____________
3. What's the weather in Miami? ____________
4. Is it hot in Chicago? ____________
5. What's the temperature in Dallas? ____________
6. What's the temperature in Seattle? ____________
7. What's the weather in San Francisco? ____________
8. Is it cold in Miami? ____________
9. What's the temperature in Detroit? ____________
10. What's the weather in Los Angeles? ____________
11. What's the temperature in Atlanta? ____________

VIII. Critical Thinking

A.

B.

Vocabulary:

relaxed	talking	worker	This person is upset.
angry/mad	proud	boss	This person is pleased.
happy	glad	listening	She is proud of her child.
worried	baby stroller	mother	He is angry at the worker.

A.	B.
1. ____________	1. ____________
2. ____________	2. ____________
3. ____________	3. ____________
4. ____________	4. ____________
5. ____________	5. ____________
6. ____________	6. ____________
7. ____________	7. ____________
8. ____________	8. ____________

UNIT 3

MONEY

How much is this? Money is necessary for many things. We buy our food. We pay our rent and bills. We go shopping. This unit is about our use of money.

Objectives

Competencies:

Ordinal Numbers
Cardinal Numbers 100—1,000,000,000
Telling Time (2)
Calendar Dates
Counting, Identifying and Using Money
Totaling Bills
Budget
Writing a Check

Structure

There Is, There Are
Present Verb
Object Pronouns: Me, You, Him, Her, It, Us, Them
Questions: Where, Which, How Much

Pronunciation:

short e (ĕ)

I. Vocabulary

A. Money

1. dollars
2. coins
3. cents
4. bills
5. wallet
6. purse
7. exact change
8. cost
9. buy
10. sell
11. expensive
12. cheap
13. budget/on a budget
14. save
15. spend
16. pay
17. count
18. cash
19. give
20. take
21. ask
22. paycheck
23. study
24. before
25. after
26. how much
27. how many
28. which
29. where
30. enough
31. rent
32. food
33. clothing
34. medicine

B. Bank

1. check
2. checkbook
3. deposit
4. savings
5. account
6. withdraw
7. teller
8. automatic teller
9. service charge

C. Time (2)

What time is it?

It's a quarter after five.

It's a quarter to ten.

It's half past two.

It's five after six.
It's five past six.

It's twenty before eleven.
It's twenty to eleven.

Exercise V-1:

What time is it?

1. ________ 2. ________ 3. ________ 4. ________ 5. ________

D. Months

January	February	March	April
May	June	July	August
September	October	November	December

Write

__________ __________ __________ __________

__________ __________ __________ __________

__________ __________ __________ __________

Exercise V-2:

January, March, May, July, August, October and December have ________ days.

April, June, September and November have ________ days.

February has ________ days and ________ every four years.

This month is ________________ . My birthday is in the month of ________________ . Christmas is in the month of ________________ . ________________ is before June. ________________ is after August. My favorite month is ________________ .

E. Ordinal Numbers

1st	first	11th	eleventh	21st	twenty-first
2nd	second	12th	twelfth	22nd	twenty-second
3rd	third	13th	thirteenth	23rd	twenty-third
4th	fourth	14th	fourteenth	24th	twenty-fourth
5th	fifth	15th	fifteenth	25th	twenty-fifth
6th	sixth	16th	sixteenth	26th	twenty-sixth
7th	seventh	17th	seventeenth	27th	twenty-seventh
8th	eighth	18th	eighteenth	28th	twenty-eighth
9th	ninth	19th	nineteenth	29th	twenty-ninth
10th	tenth	20th	twentieth	30th	thirtieth

F. Date/Calendar

March 8, 1991 / 3/8/91 / March eighth, nineteen ninety-one
December 3, 1992 / 12/3/92 / December third, nineteen ninety-two

Exercise V-3:

June 6, 1991 ______________________________

July 4, 1776 ______________________________

November 22, 1963 ______________________________

My birthdate ______________________________

A holiday in my native country ______________________________

Entrance into the United States ______________________________

Today's date ______________________________

G. Seasons

Winter	December 22—March 21
Spring	March 22—June 21
Summer	June 22—September 21
Autumn/Fall	September 22—December 21

Exercise V-4:

Spring is after ______________________.

Summer is before ______________________.

My favorite season is ______________________.

The weather here in spring is ______________________.

The weather here in summer is ______________________.

The weather here in fall is ______________________.

The weather here in winter is ______________________.

H. Cardinal Numbers 100—1,000,000,000

100	one hundred
101	one hundred and one
200	two hundred
1,000	one thousand
1,251	one thousand two hundred and fifty-one
1,000,000	one million
1,768,493	one million seven hundred and sixty-eight thousand, four hundred and ninety-three
1,000,000,000	one billion

Exercise V-5:

Listen

1. _______ 2. _______ 3. _______ 4. ______ 5. _______ 6. _______

7. ____

8. ____

I. Money

a penny = one cent = 1¢ = $ .01

a nickel = five cents = 5¢ = $ .05

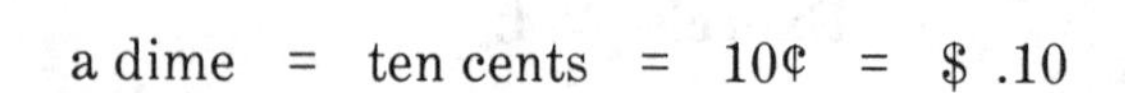

a dime = ten cents = 10¢ = $ .10

a quarter = twenty-five cents = 25¢ = $ .25

a half dollar = a fifty cents piece =
fifty cents = 50¢ = $ .50

a dollar = a dollar bill =
a buck = $1.00

a five dollar bill = five dollars =
five bucks = $5.00

Exercise V-6:

Example: 40¢ = 1 quarter 1 dime 5 pennies

1. 70¢ = ________ quarters ________ dimes
2. 95¢ = ________ dimes ________ nickel
3. $1.45 = ________ quarters ________ dimes ________ nickel
4. 30¢ = ________ dimes ________ nickel ________ pennies
5. $2.00 = ________ quarters ________ dimes

   ________ nickels ________ pennies

Exercise V-7:

Example: How many pennies are in a nickel? 5

1. How many nickels are in a quarter? __________
2. How many quarters are in one dollar? __________
3. How many dimes are in a half dollar? __________
4. How many pennies are in a dime? __________
5. How many quarters are in two dollars? __________

Exercise V-8:

Example: I have two quarters and a dime.
A cup of coffee costs 60¢.
I have enough money. I don't have enough money.

1. They have three dimes and two nickels.
   The newspaper costs 50¢.
   They have enough money. They don't have enough money.

2. Mrs. Kent has 2 dollar bills, 1 quarter and 3 dimes.
   The medicine costs $2.50.
   She has enough money. She doesn't have enough money.

3. Mr. Bet has a quarter.
   The telephone call costs 20 cents.
   He has enough money. He doesn't have enough money.

4. We have three quarters, two nickels and five pennies.
   The service charge costs $1.00.
   We have enough money. We don't have enough money.

II. Conversation

A.

Marina:	Do you have change for a dollar?
Hosein:	Sure, what do you need?
Marina:	Two quarters, three dimes and four nickels.
Hosein:	I have three quarters, a dime, two nickels and five pennies.
Marina:	That's fine.
Hosein:	Here you are.
Marina:	Thanks a lot.

B.

	1	2	3
a)	100	a camera	$70
b)	20	an electric can opener	$11.50
c)	50	a radio	$39.95

Ron: How much money is there in your purse?

Sharon: There are ____________ dollars.
(1)

Ron: Great, let's buy ____________ .
(2)

Sharon: How much is it?

Ron: ____________ .
(3)

Sharon: That's expensive. We don't need that. The food, rent, and medicine are important.

Ron: Yeah, you're right. We are on a budget.

C.

Mr. Kent:	Where is Benton's Bank?
Mrs. Fleck:	It's across the street on the corner.
Mr. Kent:	Yes, I see it.
Mrs. Fleck:	I have an account there.
Mr. Kent:	Is it easy to start one?
Mrs. Fleck:	Sure. Just ask for information there.
Mr. Kent:	Do you use checks often?
Mrs. Fleck:	I pay my bills with them.
Mr. Kent:	Thanks a lot for your help.
Mrs. Fleck:	See you later.

III. Reading

Mr. and Mrs. Larson work Monday through Friday. At the end of the month they receive their paychecks. They deposit the money in their bank account. They save for the future. They have a budget. They spend their money only on necessary things. They want a house and a university education for their children.

Exercise R-1:

1. Mr. and Mrs. Larson __________ Monday through Friday.
2. At ____________________ they receive their paychecks.
3. They deposit their money in their ____________________ .
4. They save for the ____________________ .
5. They have a ____________________ .
6. They ____________ their money only on necessary things.
7. They want a ______________ and a ______________ for their children.

IV. Structure

A. There is, There are

There is a bank on the corner.
There are many Savings and Loans in the city.
Is there a check in the envelope?
Are there twenty dollars in the wallet?

Exercise S-1:

1. There ________ four windows open.
2. There ________ a dime on the floor.
3. There ________ eight quarters on the table.
4. ________ there a checkbook on the chair?
5. ________ there three banks on this street?
6. There ________ enough money in the account.

7. __________ there an automatic teller at the bank?
8. There __________ five persons in line.
9. There __________ a wallet on the desk.
10. __________ there enough time?

B. Present Verbs

Verb: come

I come	It comes
You come	We come
He comes	They come
She comes	

He comes to work every day.
They always come late.

Verb: have

I have	It has
You have	We have
He has	They have
She has	

She has a checking account.
We sometimes have a party.

Verbs: cash, do, study

I cash	I do	I study
You cash	You do	You study
He cash<u>es</u>	He do<u>es</u>	He stud<u>ies</u>
She cash<u>es</u>	She do<u>es</u>	She stud<u>ies</u>
It cash<u>es</u>	It do<u>es</u>	It stud<u>ies</u>
We cash	We do	We study
They cash	They do	They study

Exercise S-2:

Example: (count) He <u>counts</u> the money.

1. (save) We ________________ the money every month.
2. (cash) They ________________ the check every Friday.
3. (spend) He always ________________ money.
4. (buy) You often ________________ milk at that store.
5. (sell) The store ________________ fruit every day.
6. (change) They sometimes ________________ a dollar.
7. (count) I sometimes ________________ my checks.
8. (give) They ________________ you a calendar every year.
9. (take) Rose ________________ a purse to school every day.
10. (need) Mario always ________________ change.

Write

____

____

____

C. Object Pronouns

Subject	Object
I	Me
you	you
he	him
she	her
it	it
we	us
they	them

Exercise S-3:

Example: <u>Helen</u> is a teller. I see <u>her</u> at the bank.

1. <u>Bob</u> is here every day. I always talk to ________________ .
2. <u>Karen</u> is in class. I sometimes give my notes to ________________ .

3. Mary and Sue are tellers. I see ______________ at the bank.
4. Jim and I are friends. Bob likes ______________ .
5. The movie is good. I like ______________ .
6. I go to school. The students like ______________ .
7. You and Jack are good workers. The boss likes ______________ .

Exercise S-4:

Example: (She, Her) has the money.

1. (They, Them) work at the store.
2. The store sells (they, them).
3. (I, Me) am a student.
4. The teacher sees (we, us).
5. Trong asks (he, him).

D. Questions: Where, Which, How Much

Exercise S-5:

Example: Where is the bank? It's on Primrose Avenue.
Which is the checkbook, this or that? This one is.
How much is that purse? It's twenty-five dollars.

1. ______________ is the school, this or that? That is it.
2. ______________ is the wallet? It's on the desk.
3. ______________ is this? It's fifteen dollars.
4. ______________ is the bank? It's across the street.
5. ______________ do you like, a checking account or a savings account? I like a checking account.
6. ______________ does it cost? It costs twenty bucks.

V. Writing

Mrs. Benson Friday on gets paycheck a

____

money the She deposits bank in the

____

buys She groceries

____

She rent the pays

____

budget She a is on

____

for saves She family her

____

Write

____

____

____

____

____

____

____

VI. Pronunciation

Short e (ĕ)

penny	hen	leg	pen
bed	ten	pencil	bell
check	men	desk	belt
web	jet	letter	net
egg	budget		

Listen

1. ________ 2. ________ 3. ________ 4. ________

5. ________ 6. ________ 7. ________ 8. ________

VII. Life Skills

A. Identifying Calendar Dates

NOV

S	M	T	W	T	F	S
1	2	3	4	5	6	7
8	9	10	11	12	13	14
15	16	17	18	19	20	21
22	23	24	25	26	27	28
29	30					

DEC

S	M	T	W	T	F	S
		1	2	3	4	5
6	7	8	9	10	11	12
13	14	15	16	17	18	18
20	21	22	23	24	25	26
27	28	29	30	31		

Exercise L-1:

Example: What is the date of the second Tuesday of November?
It's November 10th.

1. What is the date of the third Monday of December?

 ____

2. James has a dentist appointment on the first Monday of November. What is the date?

 ____

3. Barbara goes to driving lessons every Tuesday. How many lessons are in December?

 ____

4. December 16th is the class examination. What day of the week is that?

 ____

5. Jackie has a doctor appointment the first Monday after Christmas. What's the date?

 ____

6. Circle the date of this appointment on the calendar.

David Pasternak
Attorney-At-Law
Friday Nov. 20th 1:00

B. Totaling Bills

Exercise L-2:

Milk $1.09 Eggs $ .99 Meat $2.00 Radio $29.99

1. Alberto buys milk. He has a five dollar bill. What is the change?

   ____

2. Mrs. Sanchez buys meat and eggs. How much does she pay?

   ____

3. Giselle has 3 quarters, two dimes and two nickels. Which does she buy? ______________________________

4. Mr. Wreck buys a radio. The tax is $1.80. How much does he pay? ______________________________

C. Budget

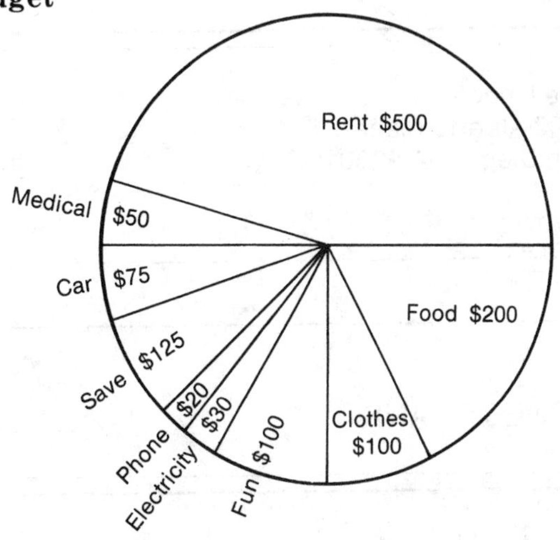

Exercise L-3:

This is the budget Thomas has planned for March. On March 1st he has his paycheck of $1200.

1. How much does he spend on food?

   ____

2. How much does he spend on housing and medicine?

   ____

3. How much is his telephone and electricity?

   ____

4. How much does he save?

   ____

Your budget:

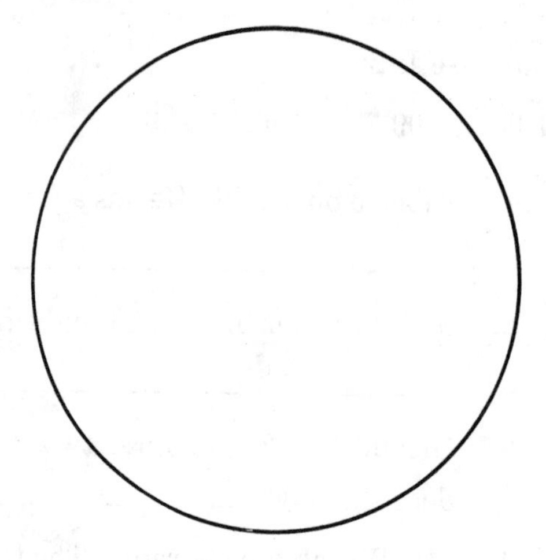

D. Writing a Check

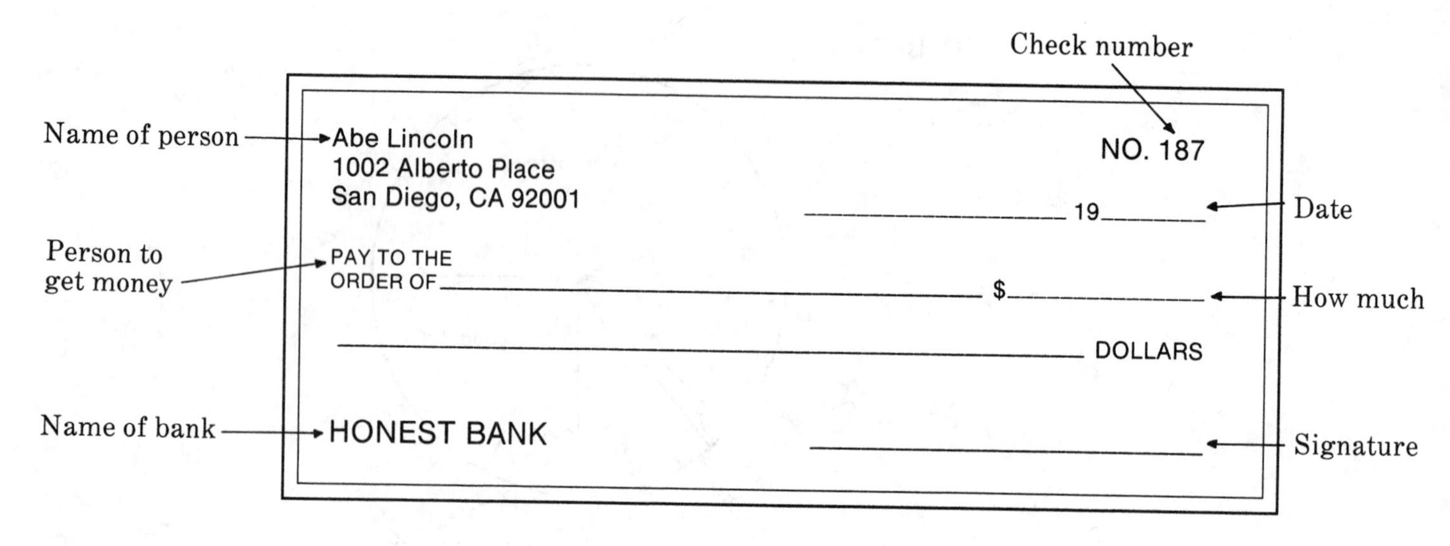

Exercise L-4:

1. Carl Rodgers pays 31.79 for a radio. He pays by check. Write the check.

Bob's Store
Date: 10-7-91

Radio	$29.99
Tax	1.80
Total	$31.79

Carl Rodgers
27 W. Broadway
Centerville, OH 40162

NO. 342

________________ 19______

PAY TO THE
ORDER OF________________________ $________

________________________________ DOLLARS

TOWN BANK ________________

2. Bianca Jagger pays $63.59 for a blouse and a pair of shoes. She pays by check. Write the check.

Nacy's
Department
Store
Date 3/14/91

Blouse	20.00
Shoes	39.99
	59.99
Tax	3.60
TOTAL	63.59

Bianca Jagger
75 Laurel Lane
Houston, TX 77032

NO. 23

_______________ 19_____

PAY TO THE
ORDER OF _______________________________ $__________

_______________________________________ DOLLARS

BANK OF THE HILLS _______________________

3. You buy ______________. It costs ______________.
Write a check.

____

NO. _______

_______________ 19_____

PAY TO THE
ORDER OF _______________________________ $__________

_______________________________________ DOLLARS

YOUR BANK _______________________

VIII. Critical Thinking

Vocabulary

She looks at the product.
The advertisement sells beer.
She is careful.
There is no price.
The market sells items.
The woman wears glasses.

It is an advertisement.
She examines the package.
She thinks about the item.
The advertisement is outside.
This is a billboard.
It is not in English.

A.

B.

A.

1. ______________________
2. ______________________
3. ______________________
4. ______________________
5. ______________________
6. ______________________

B.

1. ______________________
2. ______________________
3. ______________________
4. ______________________
5. ______________________
6. ______________________

UNIT 4

FAMILY AND COMMUNITY

How many brothers do you have? Where do your mother and father live? Is that your sister? You hear these questions about family everywhere you go. This unit is about family and also familiar places in the community like the post office, the bus station, and a restaurant.

Objectives

Competencies:

Family Members
Places in the Community

Structure

Adverbs of Frequency: Always, Often, Sometimes, Seldom, Never
Question: How Often
Present Verb, Negative and Question
Possessive: Nouns
Adjectives (My, Your, His, Her, Its, Our, Their)
Pronouns (Mine, Yours, His, Hers, Its, Ours, Theirs)
Prepositions: In, On, At, Between, Next To, Across From, On the Corner Of, In Front Of, In Back Of

Pronunciation:

Long e ($\bar{e}$)

I. Vocabulary

A. Family

1. father
2. mother
3. son
4. daughter
5. grandmother
6. grandfather
7. granddaughter/grandson
8. uncle
9. aunt
10. cousin
11. nephew
12. niece
13. parent
14. spouse
15. father-in-law
16. mother-in-law
17. sister-in-law
18. brother-in-law
19. son-in-law
20. daughter-in-law

B. Community

1. department store
2. city hall
3. hospital
4. laundromat
5. post office
6. supermarket
7. bus stop
8. drug store
9. train station
10. bakery
11. library
12. book store
13. mall
14. park
15. day care center
16. restaurant
17. health clinic
18. recreation center
19. police station
20. fire station
21. museum
22. movie theater
23. parking lot
24. employment office
25. legal aid clinic
26. church/temple
27. social security office
28. newsstand
29. bar
30. beauty salon
31. pet store
32. hospital

II. Conversation

A.

	1	2
a)	cousin	niece
b)	uncle	aunt
c)	father	nephew
d)	wife	daughter

Jerry: Good afternoon. How are you?
Nancy: Very well, thank you.
Jerry: Where's your ______________ ?
(1)
Nancy: In San Francisco at work.
Jerry: Really?
Nancy: Yes, and my ______________ is there too.
(2)
Jerry: How are they?
Nancy: They're all fine.

____

B.

	1	2	3
a)	aunt	brother	city hall
b)	sister	grandmother	the bakery
c)	cousin	uncle	the train station

Bob: Hi, how are you?
Mary: Fine. And you?
Bob: Pretty well, but my ______________ doesn't feel well.
(1)
Mary: That's too bad. I'm sorry.
Bob: She is at my ______________'s house.
(2)
Mary: Where's that?
Bob: Across the street from ______________.
(3)
Mary: I hope she gets well quickly.
Bob: Thanks.

C.

	1	2	3
a)	movie theater	bank	city hall
b)	park	fire station	movie theater
c)	hospital	library	police station

Ray: Can you tell me how to get to the ______________?
(1)
Pat: Sure. Go down one block and then turn left at the ______________, on Whitman Avenue.
(2)
Ray: Is that near the ______________?
(3)
Pat: Then go straight on that street for three blocks. Turn right for one block and it's there on your left across the street.
Ray: O.K., let's see. I go one block and turn left on Whitman, go three more blocks and then turn right, go one block and then it's across the street.
Pat: Very good.
Ray: Thanks for your help.
Pat: Don't mention it.

III. Reading

Susan works in the water department at city hall. Every day she goes to work at 8:30. On the way she walks to her grandmother's apartment to say hello. Then she buys a newspaper in front of the supermarket. She sometimes gets a donut and coffee at the cafe. Her aunt is a waitress there. She arrives at work at 9:00. Every Monday she has lunch with her husband in a restaurant. On Wednesday she has dinner with her mother. She doesn't drive. She doesn't like cars. She prefers to live close to her family and work.

Exercise R-1:

1. Susan works in the ______________________ at city hall.
2. She goes to work at ______________________ .
3. She says hello to her ______________________ at her apartment.
4. She buys a newspaper ______________________ the supermarket.
5. She sometimes gets ______________________ at the cafe.
6. Who is a waitress at the cafe? ______________________ is a waitress at the cafe.
7. When does she arrive at work? She arrives ______________ .
8. Who does she have lunch with every Monday? She has lunch with ______________________ .
9. What does she do on Wednesdays? ______________________

   ____
10. Does she like cars? ______________________
11. What does she like? ______________________

    ____

IV. Structure

A. Adverbs of Frequency: Always, Often, Sometimes, Seldom, Never

I always go to work.
The family often walks in the park.
I sometimes visit a museum.
My brother seldom watches TV.
They never buy Coke.

How often do they study? They always study.
How often do you go to a movie? I sometimes go to a movie.

Exercise: Write always, often, sometimes, seldom or never.

My brother ________________ goes shopping.
My cousin ________________ watches TV.
My uncle ________________ speaks in English.
My mother ________________ writes a letter.
My sister ________________ eats in a restaurant.

How often do you . . . ?

I always ________________.
I often ________________.
I sometimes ________________.
I seldom ________________.
I never ________________.

B. Present Verb, Negative and Question

Verb: go

I go	I don't go	Do I go?
You go	You don't go	Do you go?
He goes	He doesn't go	Does he go?
She goes	She doesn't go	Does she go?
It goes	It doesn't go	Does it go?
We go	We don't go	Do we go?
They go	They don't go	Do they go?

After -h, -s, -o, use -es.

He washes the clothes.
She passes the park.
Dan goes to work.

Change -y to -ies.

He studies the book.

Exercise S-1:

Example: (not-want) He doesn't want a ticket.

1. (not-walk) They ____________________ to school.
2. (not-drive) She ____________________ to work.
3. (not-see) I ____________________ the sign.
4. (not-know) Bert and Lisa ____________________ the direction.
5. (not-get) Linda ____________________ the newspaper.

Exercise S-2:

Example: (drive) Does he drive to school?

1. (know) ____________ he ____________ the department store?
2. (see) ____________ you ____________ the park?
3. (work) ____________ your cousins ____________ in the restaurant?
4. (practice) ____________ the students ____________ English?
5. (copy) ____________ Adrian ____________ the notes on the board?

Exercise S-3:

Example: (go) He goes to the legal aid clinic.

1. (clean) She ____________ the office.
2. (not-wash) They ____________ the clothes.
3. (watch) ____________ you ____________ TV every night?
4. (speak) ____________ Mary and Bill ____________ English?
5. (not-write) Jim ____________ letters.

6. (be) ______________ you happy?

7. (study) My uncle ______________ English.

8. (walk) She ______________ to school every day.

9. (talk) ______________ your parents ______________ to you?

10. (not-read) I ______________ the newspaper.

11. (be) He ______________ there.

12. (listen) We ______________ to the radio every week.

13. (not-cook) They ______________ on Monday.

14. (close) ______________ the store ______________ on Sunday?

15. (watch) She ______________ TV.

C. Possessive

1. Nouns

the pen of the student = the student's pen

the pens of the students = the students' pens

Exercise S-4:

Example: the car of Hal = Hal's car

1. the house of Mr. Lee

____

2. the job of Maria

____

3. the book of the student

____

4. the flag of Canada

____

5. the sign of the restaurant

____

6. the trees of the park

____

7. the parks of the states

____

8. the programs of the recreation centers

____

9. the books of the libraries

____

10. the problems of the countries

____

Exercise S-5:

Example: I like the jacket of Janet. I like Janet's jacket.

1. I like the room of my sister.

____

2. Mr. Pardee buys the fruit of that store.

____

3. Bill works at the factory of Mr. Clease.

____

4. Kevin sells the radios of those companies.

____

5. The teacher reads the papers of the students.

____

2. Adjectives

my	our
your	your
his	their
her	
its	

I have my book.
You write your name.
He has his paper.
She reads her letter.
The office has its computer.
We study our lesson.
They take their car.

Exercise S-6:

Example: I have my pen.

1. She drives __________ car.
2. He likes __________ apartment.
3. They ride __________ bikes.
4. I copy __________ notes.
5. We write __________ names.
6. The state has __________ flag.
7. You use __________ dictionary.

Exercise S-7:

Example: a. Is this Jane's pencil?
b. Yes, it's her pencil.

1. a. Is this Ben's book?

   b. Yes, it's __________ book.
2. a. Are these the students' papers?

   b. Yes, they are __________ papers.
3. a. Is that Marlene's store?

   b. Yes, it's __________ store.
4. a. Is this the hotel's restaurant?

   b. No, __________ restaurant is over there.

Write

Example: This is my eraser.

This is your __________.

That is her __________.

Is this his __________?

__________ our __________.

__________ their __________.

__________ his __________?

That is its __________.

My __________.

Our __________.

3. Pronouns

mine	ours
yours	yours
his	theirs
hers	
its	

I have my wallet. I have mine.
You sell your car. You sell yours.
He takes his pen. He takes his.
She brings her book. She brings hers.
We make our dinner. We make ours.
They have their papers. They have theirs.

Exercise S-8:

Example: a. Is this Bill's book?
b. Yes, it's his.

1. a. Is that Gloria's purse?
   b. Yes, it's ________________ .
2. a. Are those Roger's glasses?
   b. Yes, they're ________________ .
3. a. Are these their coats?
   b. No, ________________ are over there.
4. a. Where are your shoes?
   b. ________________ are here.
5. a. Are those our exams?
   b. Yes, those are ________________ .

Exercise S-9: Possessive Adjective or Pronoun

Example: This is (my, mine) pencil.

1. Those are (our, ours) books.
2. He is (my, mine) uncle.
3. That is your paper and this is (my, mine).
4. I like my house. (Their, Theirs) is beautiful too.
5. She has (her, hers) ticket. Do you have (your, yours)?

6. They like (their, theirs) job.
7. Sandra takes (her, hers) child to the day care center.
8. You have your magazine and she has (her, hers).
9. The students often talk to (their, theirs) teacher.
10. Your driver's license is here and (my, mine) is on the desk.

C. **Prepositions of Location:** In, On, At, Between, Next to, Across from, On the corner of, In front of, In back of

The students are in the class.
They live in New York.
He lives on Main Street.
The students are at school.
She lives at 109 Gandhi Drive.
He works at the factory.
The recreation center is between the park and the school.
The bank is next to the movie theater.
My cousin lives across from the day care center.
The health clinic is on the corner of 3rd Avenue and King Street.

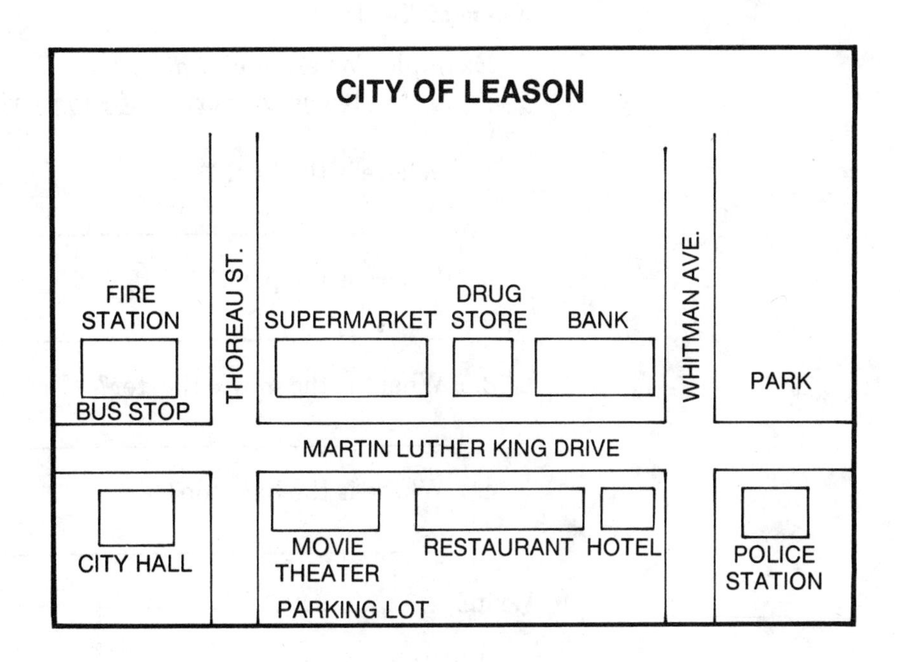

Exercise S-10:

Example: The drug store is between the supermarket and the bank.

1. The fire station is ______________ King Drive and Thoreau Street.
2. The park is ______________ the police station.
3. The restaurant is ______________ the movie theater and the hotel.
4. The bus stop is ______________ the fire station.
5. The parking lot is ______________ the movie theater.
6. Rooms are ______________ the hotel.
7. Ms. Steinheim works ______________ the bank.
8. The drug store is ______________ King Drive.
9. The police station is ______________ King Drive and Whitman Avenue.
10. The restaurant is ______________ 435 King Drive.
11. The supermarket is ______________ the city of Leason.
12. The drug store is ______________ the restaurant.
13. The movie theater is ______________ the restaurant.

Exercise S-11:

Example: Where is city hall?
It's on the corner of King Drive and Thoreau Street.

1. Where is the bank?

____

2. Where is the park?

____

3. Where is the movie theater?

____

4. Where is the bus stop?

____

Write:

I live on ______________ .

I live at ______________ .

I live in the city of ______________________.

I live across from ______________________.

______________________ is at the corner of ______________________

and ______________________.

______________________ is in back of ______________________.

______________________ is in front of ______________________.

______________________ is between ______________________

and ______________________.

V. Writing

six at Maria o'clock wakes up

____

shower takes She a

____

dressed gets She

____

her house She leaves eight at o'clock

____

gets She to at nine work

____

Write

____

____

____

____

____

And you?

I wake up at ______________________. ______________________

____

____

____

____

VI. Pronunciation

long e (ē)

key	tea	tree	sleep
bee	cheese	beans	seat
feet	three	leaf	sea
teeth	read	needle	meat
niece	teacher	between	me

1. ________ 2. ________ 3. ________ 4. ________ 5. ________

6. ________ 7. ________ 8. ________ 9. ________ 10. ________

VII. Life Skills

A. Family Members

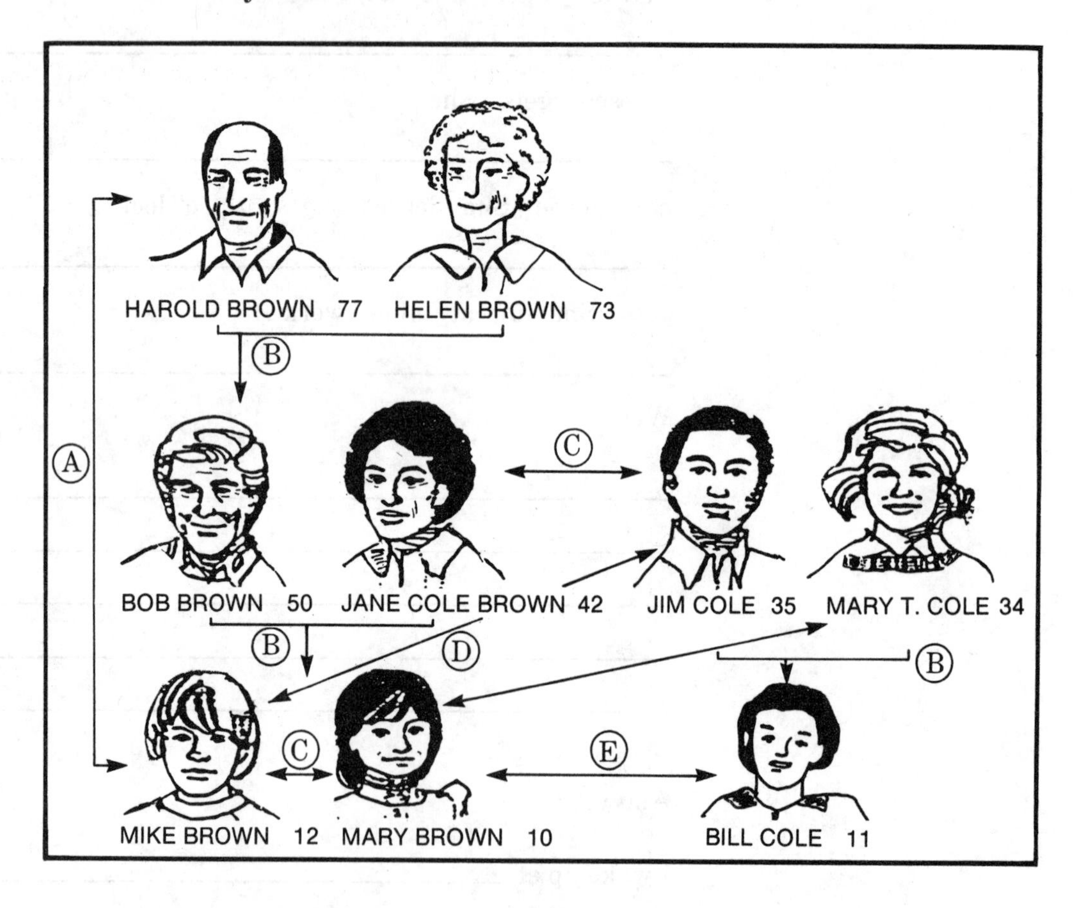

A. grandparents/grandchildren
B. parents
C. sister/brother
D. uncle, aunt/nephew, niece
E. cousins

Exercise L-1:

1. Harold Brown is the ____________________ of Mike and Mary Brown.
2. Bob Brown is the ____________________ of Jane Cole Brown.
3. Mary Brown is the ____________________ of Mr. and Mrs. Cole.
4. Bob Brown is the ____________________ of Mrs. Helen Brown.
5. Mary T. Cole is Mike Brown's ____________________.
6. Bob Brown is Jim Cole's ____________________.
7. Bill Cole and Mary Brown are ____________________.
8. Mike and Mary Brown are Mr. and Mrs. Harold Brown's ____________________.
9. How old is Mary Brown's aunt? ____________________
10. How old is Jane Cole Brown's father-in-law? ____________________

Exercise L-2: Write your own family tree.

B. Community

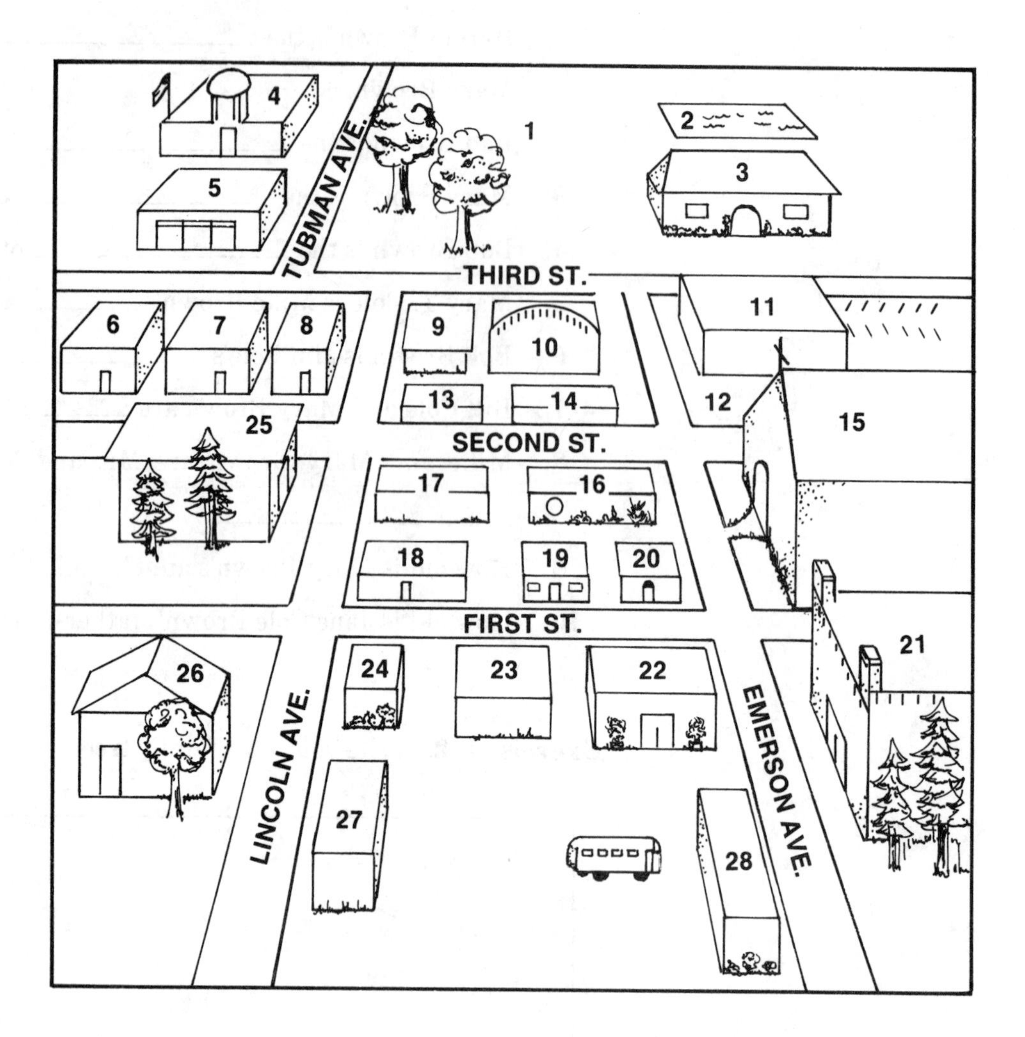

1. Park
2. Swimming Pool
3. Recreation Department
4. City Hall
5. Fire Station
6. Day Care Center
7. Laundromat
8. Post Office
9. Bakery
10. Movie Theater
11. Meegan's Department Store
12. Parking Lot
13. Liquor Store
14. Social Security Office
15. Church
16. Chinese Restaurant
17. Stationery Store
18. Legal Aid Clinic
19. Fast Food Restaurant
20. Bar
21. The Pleasing Hotel
22. Employment Office
23. Book Store
24. Bank
25. Library
26. Department of Motor Vehicles
27. Museum
28. Bus Station

Exercise L-3:

1. a. Where's the library?

   b. It's on the corner of ____________________ and ____________________.

2. a. Excuse me, where is the church?

   b. It's on ____________________ Avenue between ____________________ and ____________________.

3. a. Where can I find City Hall?

   b. It's on ____________________ Avenue right next to the ____________________ and across from the ____________________.

4. a. I'm lost. How can I get from the bus station to the post office?

   b. Go down ____________________ Avenue to ____________________ Street and turn left. Go one block. It's on the corner of ____________________ and ____________________.

5. a. My son is at the museum. How does he get to the recreation department?

   b. Easy. Just walk down ____________________ Avenue to the park and then turn ____________________ on ____________________ Street. Go one block and it's on the ____________________.

Exercise L-4:

1. Carl needs a job. He goes to the ____________________ on the corner of First and Emerson.
2. Mrs. Young likes art. She goes to the ____________________ on Lincoln Avenue.
3. Amy buys bread. She goes to the ____________________ on Third Avenue.
4. Jason mails a letter. He goes to the ____________________ on the corner of Lincoln and Third.
5. Margaret takes a bus. She waits at the ____________________.
6. Elizabeth is hungry. She goes to the ____________________.

7. Sean likes movies. He goes to the ____________ next to the bakery.
8. Angie washes clothes at the ____________ on ____________ Street.
9. Peter gets his driver's license at the ____________.
10. Frank deposits money at the ____________ on the corner of ____________ and ____________.
11. Natalie gets her library card at the ____________.
12. Richard parks his car in the ____________ on the corner of ____________ and ____________.
13. Mrs. Chung has a legal problem. She goes to the ____________ on ____________ Street.
14. Mr. Seek takes his son to the ____________ on Third Street across from the fire station.
15. Dan gets his social security card at the ____________.

VIII. Critical Thinking

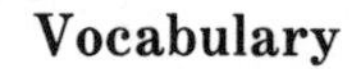

Vocabulary

less pollution	slow
many cars	no traffic problem
a crowded freeway	fast
train	more pollution
traffic problems	a train station
Many passengers are in the train.	A passenger listens to the radio.
Few passengers are in each car.	A passenger can read the newspaper.

A.

B.

A.	B.
1. ____________	1. ____________
2. ____________	2. ____________
3. ____________	3. ____________
4. ____________	4. ____________
5. ____________	5. ____________
6. ____________ ____________	6. ____________ ____________
7. ____________ ____________	7. ____________ ____________

UNIT 5

PARTS OF THE BODY

At a hospital or clinic it is necessary to know the parts of your body. You can tell doctors and nurses about where the pain or injury is. Knowing this English vocabulary is a useful tool to have at all times.

Objectives

Competencies:

Taking a Temperature
Parts of the Body and Pains
Absence Excuse for School

Structure

Articles: A/An and The
Indefinite Pronouns and Adjectives: Some, Someone, Somebody, Something, Any, Anyone, Anybody, Anything, Everyone, Everybody, Everything, No One, Nobody, Nothing
Question: Why
Review of Present Verbs

Pronunciation:

Short i (ĭ)

I. Vocabulary

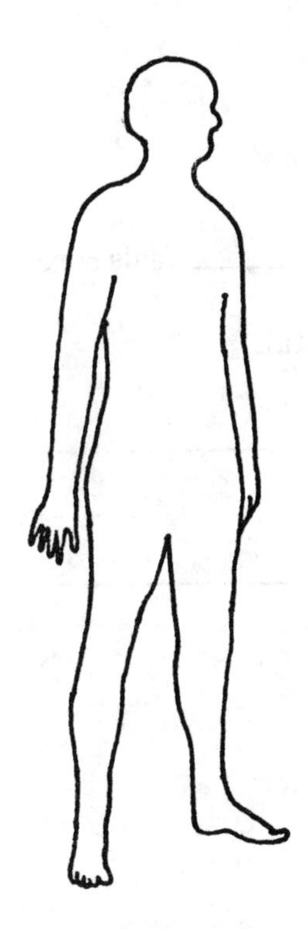

Body

1. head
2. neck
3. shoulder
4. chest
5. breasts (female)
6. arm
7. forearm
8. elbow
9. wrist
10. hand
11. fingers
12. nails
13. thumb
14. palm
15. stomach
16. waist
17. hip
18. buttocks
19. genitals
    penis (male)
    vagina (female)
20. thigh
21. leg
22. knee
23. back
24. shin
25. ankle
26. foot
27. toes
28. heel

Head

1. hair
2. face
3. forehead
4. temple
5. mouth
6. lip
7. tooth
8. chin
9. eye pupil
10. eyelid
11. eyelash
12. eyebrow
13. nose
14. tongue
15. ear
16. moustache
17. beard

Problems

1. cold
2. flu
3. headache
4. earache
5. stomachache
6. backache
7. pain
8. hurt
9. sprain
10. broken
11. sore
12. infection
13. cut
14. sunburn

II. Conversation

A.

	1	2
a)	hand	back
b)	leg	foot
c)	thumb	knee
d)	ankle	neck

Walt: How are you today?
Cleo: Not too good. My ______________ (1) feels sore.
Walt: That's too bad. My brother is in the hospital.
Cleo: Really? What's wrong?
Walt: He has a problem with his ______________ (2) .

B.

	1	2
a)	aunt	leg
b)	sister	arm
c.	mother	foot

Ken: Good evening.
Sara: Hi, Ken, what's new?
Ken: Nothing much, except for my ______________ .
1

Sara: What is it?
Ken: She's at the hospital now.
Sara: Oh, that's too bad.
Ken: It's not too serious. She has a broken ______________ .
2

Sara: I hope she gets better soon.
Ken: Thanks a lot.

C.

	1	2
a)	swim	At the community pool
b)	jog	In the park
c.	walk	In my neighborhood

Abdul: What do you do to stay healthy?
Katy: I eat right and exercise regularly.
Abdul: What kind of food do you eat.
Katy: Lots of fruits and vegetables.
Abdul: What kind of exercise do you do?
Katy: I like to ______________ .
1

Abdul: I like to do that too. Where do you do it?
Katy: ______________ .
2

III. Reading

Gilbert works for a large electronics company and he has medical insurance. When he has a medical problem, he goes to a doctor. He gets a checkup every three years. With his medical insurance, the company pays the bills. Gilbert's friend, Doug, works at a small gas station. He doesn't have medical insurance. When he feels sick, he waits and doesn't go to a doctor. He goes to a health clinic only when it is necessary. He doesn't get any checkups.

Exercise R-1:

1. Where do Gilbert and Doug work?

   ____

2. Who has medical insurance?

   ____

3. Who pays Gilbert's medical bills?

   ____

4. What does Gilbert do when he has a medical problem?

   ____

5. What does Doug do when he has a medical problem?

   ____

6. When does Doug go to a health clinic?

   ____

7. Why does Doug have no medical insurance?

   ____

IV. Structure

A. **Indefinite Articles:** a, an (for general things)

a before a consonant   an before a vowel

Exercise S-1: Write a or an.

Example: There is a hospital in that city.
There is an ambulance at that hospital.

1. There is ________ cut on your arm.
2. John has ________ appointment with Doctor Will.
3. She has ________ broken leg.
4. Your friend has ________ eye infection.

B. **Definite Article:** the (for particular things)

The hospital is next to the bank.
The ambulance is in front of his house.

Exercise S-2: Write a, an, or the.

1. There is ________ clinic in that city.
2. He has ________ broken nose.
3. Adrian has ________ ear infection.
4. There is ________ problem at ________ clinic.
5. Why do you have ________ headache?
6. ________ students are in ________ classroom.

C. **Indefinite Pronouns and Adjectives**

1.

some	any
something	anything
someone	anyone
somebody	anybody

Examples:

I have some pain in my back.
I don't have any pain in my back.
Do you have any pain in your back?
Do you have some pain in your back?
Someone is in the office.
I don't see anyone.
Does anyone know?
Does someone know?
He doesn't know anybody here.
There is somebody in the car.
Is anybody there?

Is somebody there?
There is something in my eye.
There isn't anything in the wallet.
Is anything wrong?
Is something wrong?

Any is for negative sentences.

Exercise S-3:

Example: He has (something, anything) in his hand.

1. She has (some, any) cuts on her arm.
2. They don't have (some, any) medical insurance.
3. I don't understand (something, anything).
4. (Someone, Anyone) calls the doctor.
5. I don't hear (someone, anyone).

Exercise S-4:

Gilbert has sunburn on his back, neck, and face.

Example: (arm) He doesn't have any on his arm.
(back) He has some on his back.

1. (legs) ____.
2. (face) ____.
3. (neck) ____.
4. (stomach) ____.
5. (feet) ____.

2. every — everyone
everybody — everything

Examples:

Every doctor is busy.
Everybody is here.
I talk to everyone.
She sees everything.

Exercise S-5:

Example: Everyone (<u>is</u>, are) in the class.

1. Everybody (know, knows) the answer.
2. Everything in the clinic (is, are) clean.
3. Every nurse (work, works) hard.
4. Everyone in class (is, are) smart.

Write

Every ____________________ is ____________________

______________________________________ everything .

Everyone ______________________________________

______________________________________ everybody .

3. nobody   no one
   nothing

Examples:

<u>Nobody</u> is in the clinic.
<u>No</u> <u>one</u> is there.
I feel <u>nothing</u>.

It is incorrect to use two negatives in a sentence.

He <u>doesn't</u> know <u>nothing.</u>

Use one negative in a sentence.

He doesn't know anything about medical insurance.
He knows nothing about medical insurance.

Exercise S-6:

Example: She doesn't understand (<u>anything</u>, nothing).

1. He doesn't write (anything, nothing).
2. They don't listen to (anybody, nobody) here.
3. I don't know (anybody, nobody).
4. The doctor doesn't see (anything, nothing).
5. It isn't (anyone, no one) special.

D. Question: Why?

Examples:

Why does he have a headache?
Because it's too noisy.

Why is he tired?
Because he works very hard.

Exercise S-7:

1. Why does she have a backache?

   ____

2. Why does Gary have a sore ankle?

   ____

3. Why is Mr. Jones sad?

   ____

4. Why is Ardis happy?

   ____

5. Why is Sam sleepy?

   ____

Because she has a new boyfriend.
Because she picks up many big boxes.
Because he plays soccer very hard.
Because he works all night.
Because he doesn't have money for the operation.

E. Review: Present Verb

Exercise S-8:

Example: (take) He <u>takes</u> the tablets every three hours.

1. (get) She always ______________ a stomachache.
2. (wash) The doctor ______________ his hands.
3. (not-feel) He ______________ ______________ well.
4. (take) __________ the nurse ______________ your temperature?
5. (hurt) His leg ______________ too much.

6. (not-have) She ________ ________ an infection.
7. (make) ________ you sometimes ________ an appointment?
8. (exercise) I ________ every day.
9. (be) How old ________ you? I'm twenty-nine.
10. (go) The family ________ to the clinic every month.
11. (study) The woman ________ medicine.
12. (not-get) We ________ regular checkups.

V. Writing

tired is Mary Why ?

____

hospital works She a in

____

She nurse a is

____

9 P.M. to 6 A.M. works She from

____

many She helps people

____

work busy always is She at

____

She sleep all doesn't night

____

Write

____

____

____

____

____

____

Why are you tired?

____

____

____

____

____

____

VI. Pronunciation

Short i (ĭ)

fish	hill	chin	window
eyelid	dish	chin	pick
pupil	wrist	fingers	milk
lip	infection	chicken	bill
inch	children		

Listen:

1. ________ 2. ________ 3. ________ 4. ________ 5. ________

6. ________ 7. ________ 8. ________ 9. ________ 10. ________

VII. Life Skills

A. Taking a Temperature

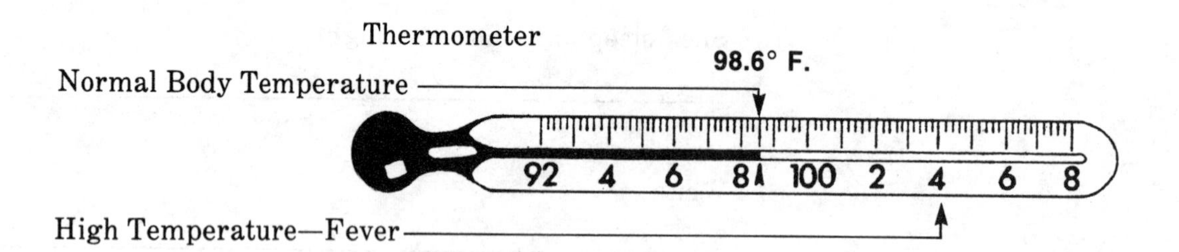

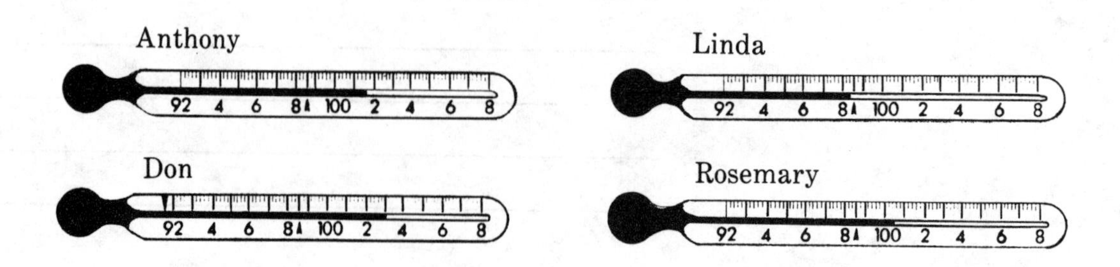

1. Who has a fever? ______________________________

2. Who has a normal temperature? ______________________

3. What is Don's temperature? ________________________

4. What is Rosemary's temperature? ____________________

5. What is Linda's temperature? ______________________

6. What is Anthony's temperature? ____________________

B. Parts of the Body and Pains

sore throat	backache	broken leg
headache	stomachache	sore feet

1. Richard eats too much. His stomach hurts. He has a

   ______________________________ .

2. Barbara walks too much. Her feet hurt. She has

   ______________________________ .

3. Edward coughs a lot. His throat hurts. He has a

   ______________________________ .

4. Penny works very hard. Her head hurts. She has a

   ______________________________ .

5. Mr. Bill carries many heavy boxes. His back hurts. He has a

   ______________________________ .

6. Ms. Cameron had an accident. Her leg hurts. She may have a

   ______________________________ .

C. Absence Excuse for School

Mrs. Hilton's son, Bruce, is sick with the flu. She writes this note to her son's teacher at school.

May 5, 19____

Dear Mr. Adam:

Please excuse Bruce from school today. He has the flu. Thank you very much.

Sincerely,

Mrs. Hilton

Your son Ted has an earache. Write a note to his teacher, Ms. Milton.

____

_______________ :

____

____

____

____

____

VIII. Critical Thinking

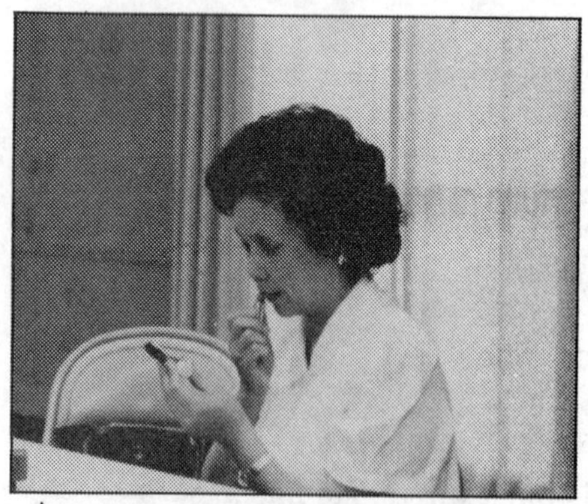

A.

B.

Vocabulary

makeup	man
body	woman
face	exercise
He is at a health club.	She puts on makeup.
He exercises.	She is at home.

A.	B.
1. ____________	1. ____________
2. ____________	2. ____________
3. ____________	3. ____________
4. ____________	4. ____________
5. ____________	5. ____________

Why does she put on makeup?

Because ____________

____

____

Why does he exercise?

Because ____________

____

____

UNIT 6

HEALTH

"If you have your health, you have everything," someone said. It's true for us today. Health is the key to our living. In this unit are health conditions, information about immunizations, and medicine labels.

Objectives

Competencies:
- Health Conditions
- Reading Medicine Labels
- Immunizations

Structure
- Present Continuous Verbs
- Adjectives
- Prepositions: In, On, Under

Pronunciation:
- Long i ($\bar{\text{i}}$)

I. Vocabulary

Conditions

1. asthma
2. bronchitis
3. cough
4. nausea
5. sprain
6. appendicitis
7. pneumonia
8. high blood pressure
9. diabetes
10. runny nose
11. throw up/vomit
12. rash
13. swelling/inflamation
14. heart attack
15. stroke
16. cancer
17. AIDS
18. venereal disease (VD)
19. tuberculosis (TB)
20. emphysema

Medicines

1. over-the-counter
2. aspirin
3. tablets
4. capsules
5. cough medicine
6. nasal spray
7. decongestant
8. antiseptic
9. prescription
10. refill
11. dosage
12. exceed

Kinds of Doctors

1. General Practitioner
2. Surgeon
3. Cardiologist
4. Orthopedist
5. Pediatrician
6. Radiologist
7. Allergist
8. Obstetrician
9. Psychiatrist

Hospital

1. symptom
2. medical history
3. blood test
4. x-ray
5. ambulance
6. healthy
7. patient
8. vaccination/ immunization

II. Conversation

A.

	1	2
a)	a terrible cough	6:15 this evening
b)	a bad allergy	1:30 this afternoon
c)	a pain in his stomach	10:45 this morning

Receptionist: Hello, Doctor Stile's office.
Mrs. Knight: Yes, this is Mrs. Knight. My son isn't feeling well.
Receptionist: Excuse me, I have another call. Can you hold for a second? Thank you. Now what was it?
Mrs. Knight: My son isn't feeling well. He has ________________ .
                                                                                    1
Receptionist: Dr. Stile is very busy today. Do you want to see another doctor or wait until tomorrow?
Mrs. Knight: I really want Dr. Stile.
Receptionist: Let me see. Well, how about ________________ .
                                                                                    2
Mrs. Knight: That's fine. We will see you then.
Receptionist: OK, thanks for calling.

B.

	1	2
a)	cold	capsules
b)	cough	teaspoons
c)	allergy	tablets

Michelle:	Please read this label for me. I don't have my glasses.
Robin:	Sure, do you have a ______________ ? (1)
Michelle:	Yes, it's really bothering me.
Robin:	The label says to take two ______________ (2) every 4 hours not to exceed 8 per day.
Michelle:	I hope this works.
Robin:	Get some rest and don't worry about it.

C.

	1	2	3
a)	chicken pox	measles	diptheria
b)	mumps	polio	tetanus
c)	measles	mumps	chicken pox

Ms. Nile:	My son is going to school this year.
Mr. Stripe:	My son, too, but now he has the ______________ (1).
Ms. Nile:	That's too bad.
Mr. Stripe:	Does your son have his immunization record?
Ms. Nile:	What's that?
Mr. Stripe:	That is the record of his protection against childhood diseases like ______________ (2) and ______________ (3).
Ms. Nile:	Really? How many are there?
Mr. Stripe:	Here is a list and a telephone number to call for more information.

III. Reading

"Hi, Kirt, what are you doing?"

"Hi, Sally. I'm watching TV."

"What are you looking at?"

"It's this medical story. You see, Mr. Rye has a heart problem and takes medicine every day. Now he is putting his medicine on the table. His young son is coming into the room while he is leaving. His son is curious. He is looking at the medicine. The tablets in the bottle are red. He is opening the bottle and holding several tablets. He is eating them. He is falling down on the floor. His father is coming into the room. He is surprised. His son is telling him about the medicine. He isn't feeling well. Mr. Rye is quickly taking him to the emergency room at the hospital."

Exercise R-1:

1. What is Kirt doing?

   ____

2. What is the TV program?

   ____

3. What kind of problem does Mr. Rye have?

   ____

4. Why does Mr. Rye's son take the medicine?

   ____

5. What mistake does Mr. Rye make?

   ____

6. Where does Mr. Rye take his son?

   ____

IV. Structure

A. Present Continuous Verbs

Present continuous verbs refer to now.

What are you doing now?

I am studying English.

Verb: work

I am working	I'm not working	Am I working?
You are working	You aren't working	Are you working?
We are working	We aren't working	Are we working?
They are working	They aren't working	Are they working?
He is working	He isn't working	Is he working?
She is working	She isn't working	Is she working?
It is working	It isn't working	Is it working?

When a verb ends with e, take away the e and write -ing.

Examples:

(take) He is taking the medicine.

(prescribe) The doctor is prescribing the drug.

Some verbs have double letters with the -ing.

Example: (stop) He is stopping.

When the verb ends with

consonant = vowel = consonant = double the last consonant

swim = swimming

plan = planning

run = running

Exercise S-1: Write the present continuous verb.

Example: (write) I am writing.

1. (talk) He ______________________________.
2. (watch) We ______________________________.
3. (make) She ______________________________.
4. (swim) They ______________________________.
5. (cry) You ______________________________.
6. (help) It ______________________________.

Exercise S-2: Write the negative form of the present continuous verb.

Example: (not-do) He isn't doing.

1. (not-come) I ______________________________.
2. (not-cough) They ______________________________.
3. (not-plan) She ______________________________.
4. (not-take) You ______________________________.
5. (not-go) We ______________________________.
6. (not-write) He ______________________________.

Exercise S-3: Write the question form of the present continuous verb.

Example: (make) Are you making?

1. (work) __________ it ______________________________?
2. (try) __________ he ______________________________?
3. (wait) __________ they ______________________________?
4. (leave) __________ you ______________________________?
5. (run) __________ we ______________________________?
6. (go) __________ she ______________________________?

Exercise: Answer with the present continuous verb.

1. What are you doing now?

____

2. What is your teacher doing?

____

3. What is your friend doing now?

____

4. What is the doctor doing?

____

Exercise S-4: Write the correct form of the present continuous verb.

Example: (work) The nurse <u>is</u> <u>working</u> at the hospital.

1. (call) He ____________________ 911 now.
2. (make) Those people ____________________ their medical appointments.
3. (check) ____________ you ____________________ the immunization list?
4. (not-come) He ____________________ to the clinic.
5. (read) Laura ____________________ the medicine label now.
6. (plan) ____________ the family ____________________ for the future?
7. (send) The hospital ____________________ the high bill.
8. (keep) The parents ____________________ the medicine out of reach of the children.
9. (not-work) The allergist ____________________ there now.
10. (examine) The doctor ____________________ the patient.

B. Adjectives

Adjectives are words that describe nouns.

Adjective	Noun	Sentence
small	car	That is a small car.
big	house	The big house is there.
tall	man	That man is tall.

Exercise S-5: Write the sentences with the adjectives and nouns.

Example: (big-hospital) It is a big hospital.

1. (strong-medicine) It is a ______________________________.
2. (big-box) The ______________________________ is on the table.
3. (nice-nurse) The ______________ is very ______________.
4. (bad-cough) That is a ______________________________.
5. (sore-throat) He has a ______________________________.
6. (hospital-expensive) The ______________ is ______________.
7. (correct-dosage) The ______________________________ is here.

Write your own adjectives.

I am looking at a ______________________________ person.

The ______________________________ hotel is in that city.

My cousin is ______________________________.

The opposites of some adjectives:

short—tall
old—young
old—new
true—false
rich—poor
full—empty
wet—dry
light—dark
fat—thin
safe—unsafe
long—short
happy—sad
soft—hard
hot—cold
noisy—quiet
high—low
heavy—light
open—closed
wide—narrow
sick—well
expensive—cheap
difficult—easy
correct—wrong
beautiful—ugly
large (big)—small
clean—dirty
fast—slow
healthy—unhealthy

Write in the correct adjective for you.

1. (long-short) My pencil is ______________________________.
2. (tall-short) My friend is ______________________________.
3. (hot-cold) I like ______________________________ weather.
4. (long-short) Breaktime is ______________________________.
5. (difficult-easy) English is ______________________________.
6. (large-small) My friend has a ______________________________ house.

7. (dirty-clean) The street I live on is ________________________.
8. (expensive-cheap) Medical care is ________________________.
9. (old-new) Your neighbor has a ________________________ car.
10. (safe-unsafe) Seat belts in cars are ________________________.

C. Prepositions: In, On, Under

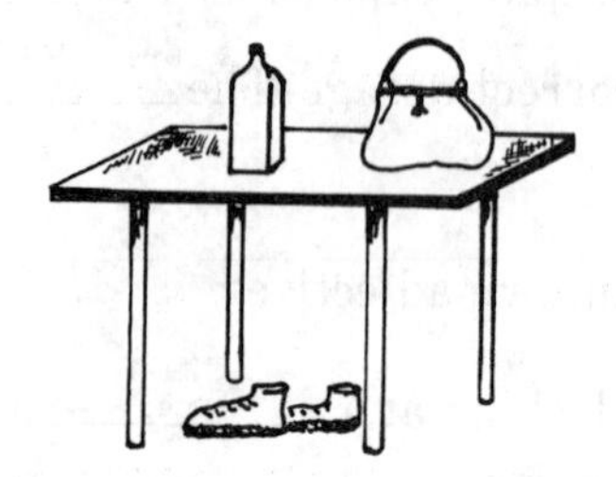

The bottle is <u>on</u> the table.
Her shoes are <u>under</u> the table.
The money is <u>in</u> her purse.

What's on your desk?

A ________________________ is on my desk.

What's under your bed at home?

________________________ is under my bed.

What's in your pocket?

________________________ is in my pocket.

What's on the teacher's desk?

____

What's in the teacher's wallet or purse?

____

What's under the teacher's paper on the desk?

____

Exercise S-6: Write on, in or under.

1. The capsules are ________________ the bottle.
2. The computer is ________________ the table.
3. He has a pain ________________ his leg.
4. His shirt is ________________ his coat.
5. The doctor's office is ________________ the second floor.
6. She is staying ________________ that hospital.
7. The river goes ________________ the bridge.
8. The bandage is ________________ his head.
9. The cut is ________________ the bandage.
10. I live ________________ a hill ________________ that city.

V. Writing

is Mrs. White healthy feeling

____

food good eats she

____

She fruits vegetables and likes

____

lots rest She of gets

____

worry too doesn't She much

____

every day exercises She

____

She walk a takes long

____

Write

____
____
____
____
____
____

How are you feeling?

____
____
____
____
____
____

VI. Pronunciation

long i (ī)

night	tie	sign	bike
dime	pie	light	smile
time	cry	eye	write
drive	high	bronchitis	appendicitis
diabetes	psychiatrist		

Listen:

1.________ 2.________ 3.________ 4.________ 5.________

6.________ 7.________ 8.________ 9.________ 10.________

VII. Life Skills

A. Conditions and Doctors

Exercise L-1: Match the doctor to the problem.

General Practitioner	Surgeon	Cardiologist
Orthopedist	Pediatrician	Radiologist
Allergist	Psychiatrist	Obstetrician

1. Al has a heart condition. ____________________
2. The small boy has a sore throat. ____________________
3. Lisa breaks her arm. ____________________
4. Mrs. Miles needs an operation. ____________________
5. Doug feels depressed and upset. ____________________
6. Carol wants a checkup. ____________________
7. Harold needs an x-ray. ____________________
8. Kyle has an allergy. ____________________
9. Mrs. Wright is pregnant. ____________________

B. Medicine Labels

Exercise L-2:

1.

Take 1 tablet three times a day for 7 days.

a. How many tablets does Claudia take every day? ____________

b. How many tablets does she take in all? ____________

2.

> Squeeze 2 or more drops into each eye as often as desired.

a. What part of the body needs this medicine? ____________

b. When does Brandon use this medicine? ____________

3.

> Directions
>
> Adults . . . 2 tablespoons
>
> Children 3 to 8 . . . 1 tablespoon
>
> Repeat this dosage every hour if needed.
>
> Do not exceed 8 doses per day.
>
> Shake well before using.

a. How many doses can Mr. Lyle take in one day?____________

b. How many doses can Timmy, age 7, take in one day? ______

c. What do you do with this medicine before you use it?

____

4.

> PEACE DRUGS
> 243 Jefferson Dr.
> Sacramento, CA 94283
>
> No. 342094
> Date: July 8, 1992 Dr. Pile
> For: Leslie Evans
>
> Take one capsule 4 times a day for 7 days.
>
> Penicillin 250 mg. #28
>
> No Refills Expires 1/93

a. Who is taking the medicine? ____________________

b. Who is prescribing the medicine? ____________________

c. What is the dosage? ____________________

____

d. What is the medicine? ____________________

e. Is it OK to use the medicine in February of 1993? ____________________

f. Is it OK to get more of this medicine? ____________________

C. Immunizations

Immunizations protect a person against diseases.
Do you have these immunizations?

	Yes	No
DTP Diptheria Tetanus Pertussis (Whooping Cough)	______	______
MMR Mumps Measles Rubella	______	______
Polio	______	______
TB Skin Test ______ Positive ______ Negative	______	______

VIII. Critical Thinking

A.

B.

Vocabulary

cigarettes	inside
outside	emphysema
alcohol	alcoholism
He is alone.	He is on the sidewalk.
They are smoking.	He is drinking alcohol.
They are talking.	They are in a cafe.
This is an unhealthy thing to do.	

A.	**B.**
1. ______________________	1. ______________________
2. ______________________	2. ______________________
3. ______________________	3. ______________________
4. ______________________	4. ______________________
5. ______________________	5. ______________________
6. ______________________	6. ______________________

7. ______________________________

How do you stop smoking?

____
____
____

How do you stop alcoholism?

____
____
____

UNIT 7

FOOD

Are you a smart shopper at the supermarket? Do you read the labels for the nutrition information? Do you have an interesting recipe? Can you read a menu in a restaurant? This unit is all about food. Eating the right food is essential for your health.

Objectives

Competencies:

Comparison Shopping
Nutrition
Recipes
Reading a Menu

Structure

Adjectives: Comparison
Nouns: Count and Noncount
Few and Less
How Much, How Many
Helping Verb: Can

Pronunciation:

Short u (ŭ)

I. Vocabulary

A. The Four Basic Food Groups

1a. Fruits

1. apples
2. pears
3. grapes
4. bananas
5. oranges
6. nectarines
7. peaches
8. apricots
9. pineapples
10. limes
11. lemons
12. cherries
13. plums
14. papayas
15. coconuts
16. mangoes
17. melons
18. watermelons
19. cantaloupes
20. strawberries
21. avocadoes
22. grapefruit

1b. Vegetables

1. lettuce
2. tomatoes
3. peppers
4. spinach
5. beans
6. broccoli
7. onions
8. cucumbers
9. potatoes
10. garlic
11. eggplants
12. corn
13. radishes
14. celery
15. cauliflower
16. artichokes
17. carrots
18. cabbage

2. Dairy Products

1. milk
2. cheese
3. eggs
4. butter
5. margarine
6. yogurt

3. Meat

1. hamburger
2. beef
3. chicken
4. steak
5. pork
6. lamb

4. Grains

1. bread
2. cereal
3. macaroni (pasta)
4. rice

B. Nutrition

1. balanced diet
2. protein
3. vitamins
4. calcium
5. carbohydrates
6. minerals
7. fat

C. Supermarket Shopping

1. checkout counter
2. cashier
3. cash register
4. aisle
5. shelf
6. groceries
7. package
8. box
9. bag
10. can
11. bottle
12. loaf
13. jar
14. pound/lb.
15. ounce/oz.
16. gallon/gal.
17. quart/qt.

D. Recipes

1. add
2. boil
3. cook
4. simmer
5. heat
6. mix
7. turn over
8. chop
9. sprinkle
10. serve/serving
11. pour
12. measure
13. measuring spoon/cup
14. tablespoon
15. teaspoon
16. frying pan
17. spatula
18. pot
19. bowl

E. Restaurant

1. appetizers
2. main course
3. soup
4. salad
5. entree
6. beverage
7. dessert
8. menu
9. waiter/waitress

II. Conversation

A.

	1	2	3
a)	vegetable	carrots and celery	chop
b)	cream	mushrooms and peppers	simmer
c)	noodle	chicken	heat

Tom: Hi, Marge, what are you doing?

Marge: I'm very busy. I'm trying a new recipe for dinner.

Tom: It smells great. What are you cooking?

Marge: I'm preparing a ______________ (1) soup with lots of ______________ (2).

Tom: Do you need some help?

Marge: Sure. You can ______________ (3) that.

Tom: I'm hungry. Let's eat.

Marge: Just wait until I finish.

B.

	1	2
a)	a head of cabbage	nectarines
b)	a couple ears of corn	bananas
c)	a bunch of carrots	oranges

Alma: Hi, how are you doing?
Tien: All right. And you?
Alma: OK. I'm shopping for this week's meals.
Tien: Are you buying some vegetables?
Alma: Yes, I really need ______________________ (1). My kids eat so much junk food. I have to give them a balanced diet.
Tien: I'm trying to eat more fruit. It's very nutritional.
Alma: The ______________________ (2) are in season now. They're delicious.
Tien: Thanks. Well, see you later.

C.

	1	2	3
a)	roast chicken	cream of tomato	filet of sole
b)	pork chops	beef barley	red snapper
c)	lamb	split pea	shrimp

Waiter: What do you want for dinner?
Mr. Dunn: I want ______________________ (1) .
Waiter: That comes with soup or salad.
Mr. Dunn: What is the soup today?
Waiter: ______________________ (2) .
Mr. Dunn: Salad with blue cheese dressing is fine for me.
Mrs. Dunn: Is your fish fresh here?
Waiter: Yes, we buy our fish every morning.
Mrs. Dunn: I want the ______________________ (3) with the soup.
Waiter: Any beverages this evening?
Mr. Dunn: Just coffee for both of us.

III. Reading

Every day Gary has a big breakfast, usually with bacon or sausage and eggs. He doesn't have lunch but he eats lots of snacks between meals. In the afternoon he has a couple of candy bars. He drinks sodas all day. When he has the chance, he goes to fast food restaurants for dinner. When he stays home, he has frozen dinners in front of the TV.

Today he is getting a physical exam and the doctor is telling him that he is overweight and his cholesterol is very high.

Exercise R-1:

1. What does Gary usually have for breakfast?

   ____

2. Does he have lunch?

   ____

3. What does he eat between meals?

   ____

4. When does he eat a couple of candy bars?

   ____

5. What does he drink all day?

   ____

6. What kind of restaurants does he like?

   ____

7. What does he eat for dinner?

   ____

8. What is the doctor telling him now about his diet?

   ____

9. What's wrong with Gary's diet?

   ____

   ____

IV. Structure

A. Comparison of Adjectives

1. Comparative: To compare two people or two things.

Adjective: tall

Sheila is taller than Lynn.

	Adjective	Comparative Form
1 sound	short	shorter
1 sound + y	busy	busier
2 or more sounds	difficult	more difficult

Examples: An apple is cheaper than a pear.
The fish is healthier than the french fries.
That cake is more delicious than this pie.

Exercise S-1:

Example: (big) His glass is bigger than yours.

1. (small) This orange is ________________ than that one.
2. (busy) The Italian restaurant is ________________ than the French one.
3. (nutritious) The juice is ________________ than the soda.
4. (high) The cake is ________________ in calories than the fruit.
5. (tasty) Your friend's spaghetti is ________________ than Barry's casserole.
6. (difficult) Her recipe is ________________ than yours.
7. (ripe) The melons are ________________ than the cantaloupes.
8. (easy) Parking is ________________ at this supermarket than the small store downtown.
9. (sweet) This grapefruit is ________________ than those.
10. (expensive) ________________ is ________________ than ________________.

2. Superlative: To compare 3 or more people or things.

Adjective: tall

Sheila is <u>tallest</u> of the three women.

Sheila

	Adjective	Superlative Form
1 sound	short	shortest
1 sound + y	busy	busiest
2 or more sounds	difficult	most difficult

Examples: The bananas are the <u>cheapest</u> fruit in the store.
For me, carrots are the <u>healthiest</u> vegetable.
That restaurant has the <u>most</u> <u>delicious</u> food in this city.

Exercise S-2:

Example: (big) That apple is the <u>biggest</u> of the three.

1. (difficult) His recipe is the ______________________ of all the recipes in class.
2. (ripe) The watermelon is the ________________ in the store.
3. (small) Limes are the ________________ fruit in the store.
4. (soft) These avocadoes are the ________________ ones here.
5. (busy) This store is the ________________ of the four.
6. (long) Their menu has the ________________ list of desserts of all the restaurants in this city.
7. (nutritious) This is the ______________________________ meal of all the meals this week.
8. (salty) That popcorn is the ________________ I know.
9. (old) That restaurant is the ________________ in town.
10. (expensive) ________________ are the ________________ fruit in the supermarket.

3. Irregular Adjectives

	Comparative	Superlative
good	better	best
bad	worse	worst

Example: This store is better than that one.
The apples are the best fruit in the supermarket.
These nectarines are worse than last year.
That is the worst restaurant in town.

Exercise S-3:

1. (good) The apricots taste ________________ than the cherries.
2. (bad) His diet is ________________ than mine.
3. (good) You are the ________________ cook in the world!
4. (bad) That was the ________________ day of my life.
5. (good) ________________ is the ________________ restaurant in the city of ________________.

B. Count and Noncount Nouns

1. Count nouns are nouns that you can count.

1 egg, 2 eggs, 3 eggs = eggs

Examples: He has a pineapple.
She has too many oranges.

2. Noncount nouns are nouns that you cannot count
cheese

Examples: He has some bread.
He has too much rice.

Most nouns are count. Here is a list of some noncount nouns:

meat	lettuce	rice	coffee
water	air	tea	salt
milk	butter	food	sugar
pepper	cheese	fruit	money
news	time	music	information
baggage	exercise	traffic	housework

Exercise S-4: Write a for count nouns and some for noncount nouns.

Example: He has a banana.

1. They have ________________ money.
2. He has ________________ dollar.
3. I want ________________ cup of coffee.
4. Ann is buying ________________ coffee at the supermarket.
5. They are getting ________________ food.
6. She needs ________________ glass of water.
7. Mrs. Trump needs ________________ water.

Exercise S-5: Write many for count nouns and much for noncount nouns.

Examples: How much baggage do you have?
The soup has too many onions in it.

1. How ________________ oranges are you buying?
2. They have too ________________ rice.
3. How ________________ time do you have?
4. How ________________ hours is the class?
5. Bruce has too ________________ salt on his food.
6. The dessert has too ________________ calories.
7. How ________________ pepper do you want?
8. Your cousins are buying too ________________ pears.
9. She is using too ________________ sugar.
10. How ________________ exercise do you do?

Few and a few are used with count nouns.

few = not many   a few = some

Examples: He has few friends. He needs more.
He has a few dollars. He can buy a pen.

Little and a little are used with noncount nouns.

little = not much   a little = some

Examples: They have little money. They need more.
They have a little money. They can buy lunch.

Exercise S-6: Underline the correct answer.

Example: He has (little, <u>few</u>) relatives here.

1. The family has (little, few) problems.
2. I want (a little, a few) sugar.
3. Gary is getting (a little, a few) mangoes.
4. Tim has (little, few) time.
5. They are eating (a little, a few) candy bars.
6. She adds (little, few) milk to the recipe.
7. The restaurant has (little, few) beverages on the menu.
8. The teacher has (a little, a few) news.
9. The supermarket sells (little, few) meat.
10. The hungry people have (little, few) food to eat.

Exercise: Write your own answers.

At the supermarket I buy too many ________________.

At the supermarket I buy too much ________________.

________________ eats too many ________________.

________________ eats too much ________________.

I drink little ________________.

I drink few ________________.

C. Helping Verb: Can

Can + regular verb

Examples: He <u>can</u> <u>speak</u> English.
I <u>can't</u> <u>eat</u> any more.
<u>Can</u> you <u>come</u> tomorrow?

Exercise S-7: Write <u>can</u> in the spaces.

Example: She <u>can</u> write English.

1. They ________________ tell you about the balanced diet.
2. I ________________ not come tomorrow.
3. ________________ you buy some peaches for me?

What can you do?

____

V. Writing

small Patricia has breakfast a

____

eats a sandwich She lunch for

____

two She glasses milk drinks of every day

____

prepares dinner well-balanced evening She a every

____

She restaurant a once month goes a to

____

junk like She food doesn't

____

Write

____

____

____

____

____

____

How about you?

____

____

____

____

____

____

VI. Pronunciation

short u (ŭ)

bus	brush	drum	nut
cup	rug	sun	gum
truck	cut	gun	bucket
jug	duck	umbrella	trunk
cucumber	lunch	pump	must

Listen:

1.________ 2.________ 3.________ 4.________ 5.________

6.________ 7.________ 8.________ 9.________ 10.________

VII. Life Skills

A. Comparison Shopping

BEST SUPERMARKET	BETH'S GROCERY STORE
Boneless New York Strip Steak $3.99/lb.	T-Bone Steak $3.69/lb.
Large Size Tomatoes $ .69	Beefsteak Tomatoes $ .59
Winston's Yogurt (8 oz.) 2 for $1	Mac's Yogurt (16 oz.) 2 for $1
Safflower Oil (48 oz.) $2.40	Heartley's Corn Oil (48 oz.) $2.00

Exercise L-1: Answer the questions.

1. Which store has the cheaper steak?

   ____

   Are the steaks the same?

   ____

2. Which store has the cheaper tomatoes?

   ____

3. Which store has the more expensive yogurt?

____

4. What is the difference between the two oils at these stores?

____

5. Mrs. Stubbs buys two pounds of tomatoes and one pound of steak at Best Supermarket. Mr. Suds buys 6 yogurts and one bottle of corn oil at Beth's Grocery Store. Who has the cheaper bill?

____

B. Nutrition

Exercise L-2: Look at the foods and write the names in the essential or not essential list.

fruit	potato chips	vegetables	cola
candy	water	grains	cookies
bread	doughnuts		

Essential Food (often)	Not Essential Food (sometimes, seldom)
______________	______________
______________	______________
______________	______________
______________	______________
______________	______________

C. Recipes

BASIC LENTIL SOUP

2 lb. lentils (or 1 lb. brown rice plus 1 lb. lentils)
2 small garlic buds, chopped
2 medium carrots, chopped
1 medium onion, chopped
2 quarts water
pinch of salt

Wash the lentils. Put into a large pot with water and salt. Bring to a boil, then simmer until the lentils are tender. Saute the chopped vegetables in a bit of oil. Add to lentils and simmer 10 minutes. Garnish with parsley. Serves 6 people.

One can add sausage if desired.

Exercise L-3:

1. What is the name of this recipe? ____________________

2. You can use lentils, or lentils and ____________________.

3. How much garlic do you use? ____________________

4. How many carrots do you use? ____________________

5. How many onions do you need? ____________________

6. How much salt do you use? ____________________

7. How many people does this serve? ____________________

Do you have a recipe?

____

____

____

____

____

____

____

____

____

D. Reading a Menu

DINO'S CAFE

Lunch Menu 11:30 A.M.—2:00 P.M.

Vegetable Soup	$ 1.50
Clam Chowder	1.75
Served with Bread and Butter	
Green Salad	$ 2.00
Shrimp Salad	4.95
Hamburger	3.95
with Cheese	4.35
Sandwiches	
Roast Beef	$ 3.50
Tuna	2.75
Avacado and Shrimp	4.00
Ham and Cheese	3.50
Meatloaf	3.50
Spaghetti	4.00
with Meatballs	5.50
Desserts	
Apple Pie	$ 2.00
Ice Cream	1.50
Beverages	
Coffee	$ .75
Tea	.65
Milk	.55
Soda	.80
TODAY'S SPECIAL: Liver and Onions	$ 4.95

Exercise L-4:

1. How much is a cheeseburger here? ______________________
2. What comes with the vegetable soup? ______________________

   ____
3. What is more expensive, a roast beef sandwich or an order of spaghetti with no meatballs? ______________________
4. How many beverages are there? ______________________
5. What's cheaper, apple pie or a green salad? ______________________

   ____
6. What is today's special? ______________________
7. Cary buys a bowl of clam chowder, a hamburger, a piece of apple pie and a glass of milk. He has ten dollars in his pocket. Does he need more money? ______________________

VIII. Critical Thinking

A.

B.

Vocabulary

beginning of a meal
plates
knife and fork
glass
cup
Boy, he's hungry.
He doesn't want any more.
so much wasted food
end of a meal
balanced meal
He is starting his dinner.
He is finishing his dinner.
He's ready to eat.

A.	B.
1. ______________________________	
2. ______________________________	
3. ____________________	3. ____________________
4. ____________________	4. ____________________
5. ____________________	5. ____________________
6. ____________________	6. ____________________
7. ____________________	7. ____________________

What do you think? ______________________________

____

UNIT 8

CLOTHING

When we buy clothing, it's wise to know the cost and sizes of clothes. Smart consumers try to find good bargains, special sales, and quality. Reading a label is a key to wearing clothes a long time.

Objectives

Competencies:

Clothing Sizes
Clothing Labels
Shopping for Clothes
Reading a Menu

Structure

Review: Present and Present Continuous Verbs
Reflexive Pronouns
Past Verbs: To Be, Regular

Pronunciation:

Past Tense -ed
Long u ($\bar{u}$)

I. Vocabulary

A. Clothing/Clothes

1. suit
2. jacket
3. shirt
4. coat
5. sleeve
6. collar
7. tie
8. vest
9. pocket
10. sweater
11. pants/slacks/
    pair of pants
12. belt
13. cap
14. hat
15. glove
16. raincoat
17. umbrella
18. shoes
19. sole
20. heel
21. skirt
22. blouse
23. dress
24. blazer
25. sweatshirt
26. jeans
27. t-shirt
28. shorts
29. underwear
30. underpants/panties
31. slip
32. bra
33. stockings/pantyhose
34. socks
35. pajamas
36. nightgown
37. slippers
38. scarf
39. sweatsuit

B. Accessories

1. jewelry
2. bracelet
3. necklace
4. earrings
5. ring

C. Store

1. department
2. rack
3. receipt
4. exchange
5. fit
6. try on
7. customer
8. salesperson
9. wear

D. Label

1. hand wash
2. machine wash
3. bleach
4. drip dry
5. line dry
6. tumble dry
7. wring
8. twist
9. dry clean
10. gentle/regular cycle
11. iron
12. cotton
13. acrylic
14. wool
15. nylon
16. permanent press

E. Colors

1. red
2. orange
3. green
4. blue
5. white
6. black
7. yellow
8. purple
9. brown

What color are your shoes? They are ____________________.

What color is your classmate's shirt? It is ____________________.

What color is the American flag? It is __________, __________

and __________.

What color is your hair? ____________________

What color are your teacher's eyes? ____________________

II. Conversation

A.

	1	2	3
a)	cousin	sweater	$19.50
b)	friend	coat	$43.87
c)	classmate	pair of socks	$4.00
d)	neighbor	handkerchief	$2.50

Jerry: Hello, how are you?
Michelle: Fine. What are you doing here?
Jerry: I'm shopping.
Michelle: What for?
Jerry: It's my ______________ (1)'s birthday and I'm looking for a ______________ (2).
Michelle: That's a nice idea.
Jerry: It costs only ______________ (3).
Michelle: That's a good price.
Jerry: Well, see you later.
Michelle: Yeah, bye.

B.

	1	2	3	4
a)	blue	medium	tight	larger
b)	red	small	loose	smaller
c)	brown	large	short	longer

Salesperson: May I help you?
Customer: Yes, do you have any ______________ (1) sweaters?
Salesperson: They are right over here. What is your size?
Customer: I take a ______________ (2).
Salesperson: Try this one on.
Customer: No, this is too ______________ (3). Do you have anything ______________ (4)?

Salesperson:	Here's one.
Customer:	Yes, this fits perfectly.
Salesperson:	Anything else today?
Customer:	No, this is it, thank you.
Salesperson:	Cash or charge?
Customer:	Cash, please.

C.

	1	2
a)	hole in	cotton
b)	rip in	nylon
c)	spot on	wool

Trudy:	Hi, Luke, what are you doing?
Luke:	I'm returning a coat to this store.
Trudy:	What was wrong with it?
Luke:	It has a ________________ (1) it.
Trudy:	That's too bad. Are you exchanging it?
Luke:	Yes. I like it. It's made of ________________ (2).
Trudy:	It's a nice design. Well, nice seeing you.
Luke:	Same here. Bye.

III. Reading

"Where are you going?" Mrs. Tonga asked Betty.

"To the mall," Betty replied.

"My husband is a compulsive buyer. He walked to the store last night to buy a pen and he returned with fifty dollars worth of things we really didn't need."

"That's too bad, Mrs. Tonga. My sister is the same way. Well, see you later."

Betty walked by herself to the mall. She needed some shoes and a new dress. She looked at women's clothes in several stores. She stopped in a store called The Fashion Place. She liked a white and blue dress. She tried it on. It fit very nicely. She purchased it. She was very tired and then walked home. She didn't buy any shoes.

The next day she noticed a hole in the dress. She returned it to the store and exchanged it for another one.

Exercise R-1:

1. What kind of shopper is Mr. Tonga?

   ____

2. Who walked with Betty to the mall?

   ____

3. What did she want to buy?

   ____

4. Where did she shop?

   ____

5. What did she try on?

   ____

6. How did the dress fit?

   ____

7. Why didn't she buy shoes?

   ____

8. What was wrong with the dress?

   ____

9. What did she do?

   ____

IV. Structure

A. Review: Present Continuous and Present Verbs

Exercise S-1: Write the present and present continuous of the verbs.

Example: (shine) I never <u>shine</u> my shoes but today I'm <u>shining</u> them.

1. (study) They never ______________ but today they ______________ because they have an exam.
2. (rent) He seldom ______________ a tuxedo but today he ______________ one because he is getting married.
3. (wear) She often ______________ a dress but today she ______________ pants.

4. (buy) You sometimes ______________ socks but today you ______________ slippers.
5. (wash) We always ______________ the shirts but today we ______________ the pants.

I always ______________ but today I ______________ ______________.

Exercise S-2: Write present and present continuous verbs.

Example: a. Why are you shopping for clothes today?
b. I'm shopping for clothes because I need a suit.
I usually shop on Saturdays.

1. a. Why are you sewing?
   b. I ______________ because I ripped my dress.
   I never ______________ before work.
2. a. Why is your brother wearing white shoes?
   b. He ______________ because he likes them.
   He always ______________ white shoes.
3. a. Why are the students studying so hard?
   b. They ______________ because they have an exam this afternoon.
   They usually ______________ on Tuesday mornings.
4. a. Why are you walking to school?
   b. I ______________ because I don't want to pollute the air.
   I often ______________ to school.

B. Reflexive Pronouns

myself	ourselves
yourself	yourselves
himself	themselves
herself	
itself	

Reflexive pronouns refer back to the subject.

Examples: I cleaned the closet by myself.
She moved the rack of clothes by herself.
They studied by themselves.

Exercise S-3: Write the reflexive pronouns.

1. We were proud of ______________.
2. I sewed the shirt by ______________.
3. The boy tried on the pants by ______________.
4. They go to the shoemaker by ______________.
5. She fixed the button by ______________.
6. Did you look at ______________ in the mirror?
7. The machine stops by ______________.

What do you do by yourself?

____

C. **Past Verb: To Be**

I was	I wasn't	Was I?
You were	You weren't	Were you?
He was	He wasn't	Was he?
She was	She wasn't	Was she?
It was	It wasn't	Was it?
We were	We weren't	Were we?
They were	They weren't	Were they?

Exercise S-4: Write in the past form of the verb to be.

Example: I was here yesterday.

1. We ______________ at the mall last Wednesday.
2. The jacket ______________ too tight.
3. ______________ you in the men's department a few minutes ago?
4. (negative) He ______________ happy with his new shoes.
5. The overcoat ______________ in the closet.
6. Which ______________ your slippers?
7. The students ______________ in the classroom.

8. ________________ he in the fitting room?

9. Glenda ________________ at work yesterday.

10. (negative) I ________________ at home last Saturday.

Where were you yesterday?

____

Why were you upset?

I __________ upset because ________________________________ .

D. **Past Verbs: Regular**

Verb—return

I return	I didn't return	Did I return?
You return	You didn't return	Did you return?
He returns	He didn't return	Did he return?
She returns	She didn't return	Did she return?
It returns	It didn't return	Did it return?
We return	We didn't return	Did we return?
They return	They didn't return	Did they return?

Exercise S-5: Write the past tense of the verb.

Example: (try) She tried on the blouse.

1. (sew) Henry ________________ the rip in his pants.
2. (tie) The girl ________________ her tennis shoes.
3. (wash) They ________________ their clothes yesterday.
4. (button) I ________________ up my shirt.
5. (zip) She ________________ up her zipper.
6. (fix) The shoemaker ________________ our shoes.

Exercise S-6: Write the negative of the past verb.

Example: (dress) The uncle didn't dress the baby.

1. (clean) The dry cleaners ______________ his suit very well last week.
2. (turn) Sara ______________ on the washing machine.
3. (exchange) I ______________ the sweater with the hole in it for a new one.
4. (receive) We ______________ a call.
5. (look) They ______________ around for a long time.

Exercise S-7: Write the question of the past verb.

Example: (try) Did she try on the dress?

1. (like)__________ you __________ your pair of pants?
2. (iron)__________ they __________ their clothes?
3. (wash)__________ George __________ his socks?
4. (rinse)__________ the washing machine __________ the clothes?
5. (tie)__________ Mr. Soon __________ his tie?

Exercise S-8: Write the correct forms of the past tense verbs.

Example: (return) He returned home immediately.

1. (want) The jeweler ______________ to show you some special rings.
2. (attend)__________ the students __________ class?
3. (not-use) Sandra ______________ her umbrella.
4. (clean) __________ the dry cleaners __________ your suit?
5. (plan) The family ______________ their trip.
6. (not-ask) She ______________ for a diamond ring.
7. (open) When __________ the store __________?
8. (not-need) They ______________ those clothes.

9. (exchange) Barbara ______________________ the gloves.

10. (purchase) Ed ____________________ several pairs of pants.

V. Writing

department store Mr. Moody last walked to the by Tuesday himself

____

clothes He looked men's at

____

tried pair pants He on grey a of

____

fit well They very

____

They on sale were

____

paid them cash with for He

____

himself He home by returned

____

Write

____

____

____

____

____

____

What clothes did you purchase?

____

____

____

____

____

____

VI. Pronunciation

Regular Past Tense (-ed)

1. After verbs that end in t or d, pronounce "id."

   (t) wanted painted rented
   (d) needed faded ended

2. After verbs that end in f, k, p, s, ch, sh, x, pronounce "t."

   (f) stuffed coughed
   (k) worked looked
   (p) stopped shopped
   (s) dressed danced
   (ch) watched matched
   (sh) washed cashed
   (x) mixed fixed

3. After verbs that end in b, g, j, l, m, n, r, v, z and the a, e, i, o, u sounds, pronounce "d."

   (b) robbed rubbed
   (g) dragged drugged
   (j) judged raged
   (l) called billed
   (m) timed seemed
   (n) cleaned warned
   (r) erred marred
   (v) lived saved
   (z) razed hazed
   (a) played stayed
   (e) studied carried
   (i) cried tried
   (o) owed sewed
   (u) chewed sued

Pronounce these past tense verbs now:

complained	loaded	kissed
boiled	traded	taxed
towed	entered	added
wished	closed	rated

long u ($\bar{u}$)

huge	suit	fruit	tube
mule	cube	tool	noon
moon	do	cute	blue
due			

Listen:

1.________ 2.________ 3.________ 4.________ 5.________

6.________ 7.________ 8.________ 9.________ 10.________

VII. Life Skills

A. Sizes

Women

Small (size 6—10)
Medium (size 12—14)
Large (size 16—18)
Extra Large (size 20—22)

Dresses, skirts, blouses, pants, and suits:
6 8 10 12 14 16 18 20

Junior sizes:
5 7 9 11 13

Underwear:
Bras:
32 34 36 38 (A, B, or C)
Slips:
small, medium, large
short, medium, long

Shoes, boots, slippers, tennis shoes:
5 6 7 8 9 10

Men

Small
Medium
Large
Extra Large

Shirts:
Neck: 14 15 16 17
Sleeve: 31 32 33 34 35 36

Suits, coats, jackets, pants, jeans:
32 34 36 38 40 42 44
(regular and long)

Shoes, boots, slippers, tennis shoes:
5 6 7 8 9 10 11 12 13

Exercise L-1: Choose the correct answer.

1. Rosa wears a size 6. It's ____________.
   a. small b. large c. medium
2. Mr. Toscanni's shirt neck size is 15 and the sleeve is ____________.
   a. 10 b. 32 c. 65
3. Sara's skirt is size ____________.
   a. 32 b. 56 c. 10
4. John's boots are size 13. They are ____________.
   a. small b. large c. medium
5. Tina's tennis shoes are size 5. They are ____________.
   a. small b. large c. medium
6. Mrs. Long buys a 34B ____________ and a ____________ slip.
   a. small/long b. bra/medium c. bra/34B

B. Labels

1. shirt
MACHINE WASH
NO BLEACH
TUMBLE DRY

2. sweater
HAND WASH
COOL WATER

3. coat
DRY CLEAN
ONLY

4. blouse
DO NOT DRY CLEAN
HAND WASH
COLD WATER ONLY
DRIP DRY

5. jeans
MACHINE WASH
LINE DRY

Exercise L-2: Answer yes or no.

1. You wash the sweater in the washing machine. ________
2. You take the coat to the dry cleaners. ________
3. You use bleach with the shirt. ________
4. You use hot water for the blouse. ________
5. You wash the jeans in the washing machine. ________
6. You take the blouse to the dry cleaners. ________
7. You dry the jeans on a clothes line. ________
8. You tumble dry the shirt in the dryer. ________

What does a clothing label of your classmate say?

____

C. Shopping for Clothes

Reg. 25.00 Now 18.99
Leather Casual Shoes
White, Black, Red, Yellow
Women's 5½ to 9

Cotton Dress Socks
4 pairs 13.00

Men's Knit Shirt
Easy Care Polyester/Cotton
Choose from 12 Colors
2 / 17.00

Leebock Tennis Shoes
Men or Women's
White or Black
Reg. 46.95 Now 37.99

Prices Effective Thru May 8

Exercise L-3:

1. What is the men's shirt made of? ____________________

   ____

2. How much is one pair of socks? ____________________
3. How much is a pair of tennis shoes? ____________________
4. What colors are the women's casual shoes? ____________________

   ____

   What are they made of? ____________________
5. How much is one knit shirt? ____________________
6. What colors are the tennis shoes? ____________________
7. Mary wears a size 10 shoe. Can she buy some leather casual shoes? ____________________
8. The Wilson family is going shopping on May 10th. Are these prices the same at that time? ____________________
9. How many colors can you choose from the men's shirts? ________
10. Mrs. Shu's son has new tennis shoes. Her son wants a pair of Leebock's tennis shoes now because all his friends have those tennis shoes. What does she say to her son?
    a. We don't waste money just for your friends. You already have new tennis shoes.
    b. Here's $50. Go buy them.
    c. When these shoes are old, we will buy them. Not now.
    d. ____

VIII. Critical Thinking

A.

B.

Vocabulary

clothing racks
He needs.
donation truck
She can afford new clothes.
He can't afford new clothes.
She gives clothing to a second-hand store.
He is shopping at the second-hand store.
recycling clothing
She doesn't need.
He walked to the store.
She cleaned out her closet.

A.	**B.**
1. ____________________	
2. ____________________	2. ____________________
3. ____________________	3. ____________________
4. ____________________	4. ____________________
5. ____________________ ____________________	5. ____________________ ____________________
6. ____________________ ____________________	6. ____________________ ____________________

UNIT 9

HOUSING

Did you live in a nice house when you were small? Where do you live now? This unit is about where we live. We will study about finding a good place to live and having the right furniture there.

Objectives

Competencies:

Reading Housing Ads
Floor Plans for a House
Shopping for Household Items

Structure

Past Verbs: Irregular
Prepositions: With, For, Of
Helping Verb: Should

Pronunciation:

Short o (ŏ)

I. Vocabulary

A. Kinds of Houses

1. house
2. duplex
3. mobile home
4. apartment
5. townhouse
6. condominium

B. Rooms of a House

1. living room
2. kitchen
3. bathroom
4. dining room
5. hall
6. bedroom
7. study
8. den/family room
9. basement
10. attic
11. closet
12. garage
13. patio
14. backyard

C. Furniture

1. sofa
2. coffee table
3. table
4. lamp
5. rug/carpet
6. chairs
7. armchair
8. desk
9. bookcase
10. mirror
11. stove/range/oven
12. refrigerator
13. bed
14. pillow
15. blanket
16. sheets
17. washer

(continued)

18. dryer
19. television
20. VCR
21. sewing machine
22. computer
23. stereo
24. plate
25. cup
26. saucer
27. silverware
28. knife
29. fork
30. spoon
31. glass
32. napkin

D. Apartment

1. lobby
2. balcony
3. stairs
4. fire escape
5. storage
6. laundry room
7. floor
8. elevator

Newspaper Abbreviations

1. furn = furnished
2. unfurn = unfurnished
3. apt = apartment
4. AEK = all electric kitchen
5. avail = available
6. balc = balcony
7. bldg = building
8. BR = bedroom
9. condo = condominium
10. cpt = carpet
11. drps = drapes
12. din = dining room
13. dep = deposit
14. dw = dishwasher
15. exc = excellent
16. flrs = floors
17. fplc = fireplace
18. frig = refrigerator
19. gar = garage
20. htd = heated
21. hdwd = hardwood floors
22. hw = hot water
23. incl = includes
24. kit = kitchen
25. cur = curtains
26. refrig = refrigerator
27. pkg = parking
28. lge = large
29. lndry = laundry
30. mo = month
31. mod = modern
32. nr = near
33. nudec = new decoration
34. renov = renovation
35. rm = room
36. refs = references
37. sgl = single
38. spec = spectacular
39. stu = studio
40. stv = stove
41. trans = transportation
42. util = utilities
43. w/d = washer/dryer
44. wk = week
45. vw = view
46. w/w = wall to wall
47. yd = yard

II. Conversation

A.

	1	2
a)	a house	small
b)	an apartment	narrow
c)	a duplex	little

Thad: Good evening, how are you?
Jane: Fine, and how about you?
Thad: Not bad. Where are you going?
Jane: I'm going home.
Thad: Where do you live?
Jane: In ______________(1) in the city of Millbrae.
Thad: When did you move there?
Jane: A few months ago. It's very comfortable. It has a big kitchen, a dining room, two bedrooms and a bathroom.
Thad: Sounds nice.
Jane: There's also a garage but it's ______________(2).

B.

	1	2	3
a)	$800	$200	a garage
b)	$750	$300	laundry facilities
c)	$900	one month's rent	storage space

Bob: Hello, I'm calling about the ad for the apartment.
Mr. Cox: Yes, it's still available.
Bob: How much is the rent?
Mr. Cox: It's ______________(1) a month with ______________(2) deposit.
Bob: How many rooms are there?
Mr. Cox: There are four—2 bedrooms, a living room and a kitchen.
Bob: Does it have ______________(3)?
Mr. Cox: Yes it does. And it also has a central location. It's near transportation, stores and schools.
Bob: Can I come and see it?
Mr. Cox: Sure. How about 1 P.M.?
Bob: That's fine. See you then.

C.

	1	2	3	4
a)	The faucet is leaking	landlord	is he	He fixes
b)	The ceiling is cracked	landlady	is she	She fixes
c)	The toilet doesn't work	managers	are they	They fix
d)	The sink is clogged up	manager	is he	He fixes

Carlos: What's wrong?

Angie: ________________ (1) .

Carlos: You should tell the ________________ (2) .

Angie: Where ________________ (3) ?

Carlos: In apartment 12. ________________ (4) those things.

Angie: Thanks for telling me.

III. Reading

Ralph lived in a quiet place in the country and then moved to the city. It seemed crowded and there were many homeless people on the street. He looked for an apartment in the newspaper. The rents were very high. He called an old friend, Kevin. Kevin told him that his brother had a nice, large apartment and he needed a roommate. Ralph went to the apartment and met Kevin's brother, James. They liked each other and decided to be roommates. They shared the apartment and the rent.

Exercise R-1:

1. Where did Ralph live first?

   ____

2. Where did he move to?

   ____

3. What was different about the city?

   ____

4. Where did he look for an apartment?

   ____

5. What was wrong with the apartments?

   ____

6. Who did he call?

____

7. Who needed a roommate?

____

8. How did Ralph solve the problem of finding a cheap place to live?

____

____

IV. Structure

A. Past Tense of Irregular Verbs

Verb: go

I went	I didn't go	Did I go?
You went	You didn't go	Did you go?
We went	We didn't go	Did we go?
They went	They didn't go	Did they go?
He went	He didn't go	Did he go?
She went	She didn't go	Did she go?
It went	It didn't go	Did it go?

Here is a list of regular past tense verbs:

drink - drank	blow - blew	break - broke
sink - sank	grow - grew	wake - woke
shrink - shrank	know - knew	speak - spoke
sing - sang	throw - threw	choose - chose
ring - rang	draw - drew	drive - drove
swim - swam	fly - flew	freeze - froze
come - came	see - saw	ride - rode
run - ran	bend - bent	write - wrote
give - gave	send - sent	wear - wore
do - did	fall - fell	steal - stole
go - went	bleed - bled	take - took
get - got	lead - led	shake - shook
build - built	meet - met	sell - sold
leave - left	feed - fed	tell - told
keep - kept	hold - held	say - said
feel - felt	eat - ate	pay - paid

(continued)

mean - meant	spend - spent	begin - began
bring - brought	hang - hung	lie - lay
buy - bought	lose - lost	lay - laid
catch - caught	make - made	hide - hid
fight - fought	sit - sat	sleep - slept
teach - taught	stand - stood	sweep - swept
hear - heard	win - won	wind - wound
find - found		

Note: The past tense of some irregular verbs doesn't change.

put - put	cost - cost	cut - cut
fit - fit	had - had	hit - hit
hurt - hurt	let - let	quit - quit
read - read	set - set	shut - shut
spread - spread		

Exercise S-1: Write the past tense of the verb.

Example: (fly) They <u>flew</u> to L.A. last week.

1. (read) He ________________ the ad in the newspaper last night.
2. (find) She ________________ an apartment yesterday.
3. (drive) They ________________ downtown.
4. (get) I ________________ the key to the apartment.
5. (begin) We ________________ cleaning two days ago.

Exercise S-2: Write the negative past tense of the verb.

Example: (eat) I <u>didn't</u> <u>eat</u> at home last night.

1. (set) The kids ____________________ the table.
2. (sleep) My cousin ____________________ in the condominium.
3. (catch) We ____________________ the bus.
4. (feel) She ____________________ well.
5. (cut) I ____________________ myself badly in the sink.

Exercise S-3: Write the question using the past tense of the verb.

Example: (write) Did he write a note to the landlord?

1. (spend) ____________ they ____________ a lot on furniture?
2. (meet) ____________ you ____________ her at the open house?
3. (feed) ____________ he ____________ the baby?
4. (see) ____________ Nick ____________ the duplex?
5. (freeze) ____________ your friend ____________ the fish?

Exercise S-4: Write the past tense forms of the verbs.

Example: (take) He took my pen.

1. (sweep) ____________ she ____________ the back yard?
2. (spread) The boy ____________ butter on his bread.
3. (lose) Their team ____________ the game yesterday.
4. (not-keep) I ____________ the receipt.
5. (build) He ____________ their house five years ago.
6. (give) ____________ he ____________ you the key?
7. (not-grow) The city ____________ very much.
8. (wake) I ____________ up late this morning.
9. (make) ____________ the family ____________ their beds?
10. (not-hear) Gretchen ____________ anything.

Exercise: Write your answers with the past tense.

1. What did you wear yesterday?

   ____

2. When did you lie down yesterday?

   ____

3. What did you lay on the table?

   ____

4. What did you hang in your closet last night?

   ____

5. What did you do yesterday?

____

6. What did you do a month ago?

____

7. What did you do last year?

____

B. Prepositions: With, For, Of

Examples: Mr. Peters went <u>with</u> his wife to the apartment.
That bedroom is <u>for</u> their daughter.
The roof <u>of</u> their duplex is very old.

Exercise S-5: Write with, for or of.

Example: She came <u>with</u> her mother.

1. The size ____________ her house is very big.
2. The utilities bill is ____________ them.
3. I walked ____________ my friend around the block.
4. That closet is ____________ his wife.
5. Terry drove ____________ me to the store.
6. The price ____________ the house is too high.
7. The package is ____________ you.
8. Storage space is available ____________ you.
9. The driveway ____________ that house is long.
10. Did he go ____________ you to enjoy the view?

C. Helping Verb: Should

Should is for obligation, advice or opinion.

Examples: You <u>should</u> cross the street carefully.

He <u>should</u> go to that movie.
You <u>should</u> rent an apartment in my neighborhood.

Exercise S-6: Write the helping verb should in the spaces.

Example: I should call my mother.

1. They ______________________ study more.
2. Catherine ______________________ get more sleep.
3. The Wilson's ______________________ move to that other city.
4. The child ______________________ cross the street at the signal.
5. He ______________________ pay his rent on time.

Exercise: Write your own answers with should.

Example: The child should eat good food.

1. The student should ______________________.
2. The teacher should ______________________.
3. The policeman should ______________________.
4. My brother should ______________________.
5. My friend should ______________________.
6. The government should ______________________.

V. Writing

apartment Mrs. Sun an looked for

____

newspaper found She the in one

____

it She likes

____

big kitchen The is modern and

____

room view living a has The

____

There garage any isn't

____

location It in a good is

____

The quiet is neighborhood

____

Write

____

____

____

____

____

____

How about you?

____

____

____

____

____

____

VI. Pronunciation

short o (ŏ)

clock	box	lock	rob
fog	ox	bottle	socks
pot	block	log	top
rock	spot	hot	rocket
mop	dock		

Listen:

1.________ 2.________ 3.________ 4.________ 5.________

6.________ 7.________ 8.________ 9.________ 10.________

VII. Life Skills

A. Newspaper Ads for Housing

5010-FURNISHED APARTMENTS	5020-UNFURNISHED APARTMENTS	5030-UNFURNISHED HOUSES
SAN CARLOS 1 BR, cpts, close to trans. No pets. $650 555-7685	DALY CITY 2 BR, 1 BA, lndry, encl. parking, secure bldg. $625 555-7986	BELMONT lrg 3 BR, 2 BA, mod, hdwd, fplc, stv, frig, yd, spec vw. Refs. $1095 Contact agent George Bell 555-0987
BELMONT $725 and Up. 1, 2 and 3 BRs, AEK, d/w, drps, pool, vw, balcony, elevators, 200 Davey Glen Road	PACIFICA stu, new cpt, incl. util, avail now $595 555-4573	

Exercise L-1:

1. In the newspaper, the number 5010 is for ____________ apartments.
2. Gary wants to rent a studio in Pacifica for under $700. What phone should he call? ____________
3. Mrs. Townson can't rent the apartment in ____________ because she has a cat.
4. Which is cheaper, the furnished apartment in San Carlos or the unfurnished one in Daly City? ____________
5. Do all of the furnished apartments at 200 Davey Glen Road rent for $725? ____________
6. Who do you call about the unfurnished house in Belmont?

   ____
7. Which of the above buildings has a fireplace? ____________
8. Does the unfurnished apartment in Daly City have a place to wash and dry clothes? ____________
9. Mrs. Garp is moving to Daly City. She is alone and wants a safe place to live. What number should she call? ____________
10. What's good about the furnished apartment in San Carlos? ____________

    ____

B. Floor Plan of a House

Here is a floor plan of a house.

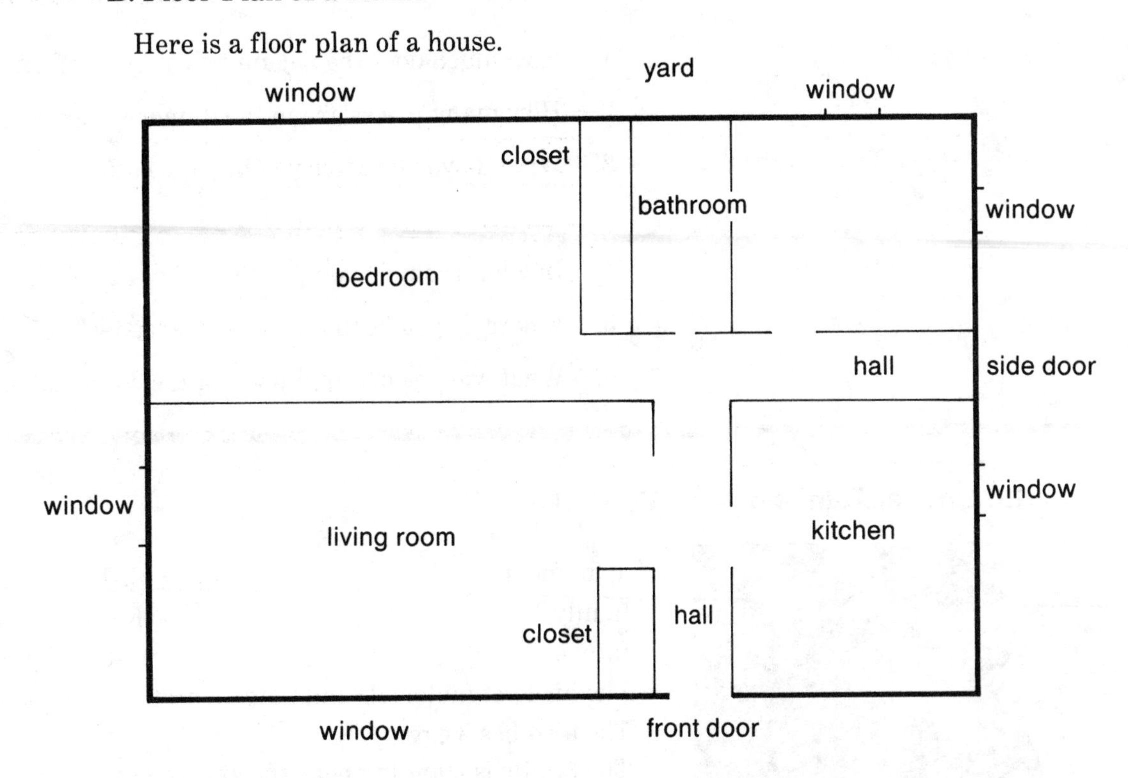

What was the floor plan of the house you were in as a child?

C. Shopping for Household Items

Bedina Vacuum Cleaner $64.88 Lightweight	Coffee Table 15H x 49W x 18D" Oak Finish Assembly Required Reg 44.99 Now 29.99	$39.00 21 pc corning dinnerware set 4 ea: dinner plates, salad plates, bowls, cups, saucers, 1 qt. bowl

Exercise L-2:

1. How much does the vacuum cleaner cost? ____________
2. How many pieces are in the dinnerware set? ____________
3. What do you do after you buy the coffee table? ____________
   ____
4. In what room do you put the coffee table? ____________
5. Where do you keep the vacuum cleaner? ____________
6. What was the original price of the coffee table? ____________

VIII. Critical Thinking

A.

B.

Vocabulary

apartment	bird
family	shelter
future	nest

The bird got materials and made a nest.
The bird has 3 eggs
The family is standing near the apartment.
They found an apartment and moved in.

A.	B.
1. ____________	
2. ____________	
3. ____________	3. ____________
4. ____________	4. ____________
5. ____________	5. ____________
6. ____________	6. ____________
7. ____________	7. ____________

Do we all need shelter? ____________

____

____

____

UNIT 10

JOBS

This unit is about the world of work. It's important to find a good job and know how to apply for it. Life is a lot better when you enjoy a job in a safe and fair situation.

Objectives

Competencies:

Finding a Job in the Want Ads
Filling out a Social Security Application
Job Application

Structure

Review of Verbs in the Past Tense
Future Verbs: Will
Too

Pronunciation:

Long o ($\bar{o}$)

I. Vocabulary

A. Kinds of Jobs

1. custodian
2. construction worker
3. mechanic
4. bricklayer/mason
5. carpenter
6. house painter
7. truck driver
8. bus driver
9. taxi driver
10. welder
11. electrician
12. plumber
13. assembler
14. police officer
15. security guard
16. clerk
17. receptionist
18. accountant/bookkeeper
19. lab technician
20. engineer
21. housekeeper
22. lawyer
23. architect
24. teacher
25. journalist
26. artist
27. photographer
28. baker
29. chef/cook
30. florist
31. waiter/waitress
32. butcher
33. letter carrier
34. busboy
35. firefighter
36. nurse
37. doctor
38. dentist
39. scientist
40. pharmacist
41. hairdresser
42. model
43. newscaster

(continued)

44. grocer
45. manager/supervisor
46. salesperson
47. typist
48. secretary
49. farmer
50. data processor
51. tailor
52. gas station attendant

B. Workplace

1. salary/pay
2. wages
3. earn
4. experience/background
5. benefits
6. paid holidays
7. vacation
8. health insurance
9. sick leave
10. schedule
11. promotion
12. raise
13. break
14. shift (day, swing, night)
15. union
16. application
17. resume
18. employed/unemployed
19. position
20. opening
21. full-time/part-time
22. overtime
23. employer
24. employee
25. paycheck

II. Conversation

A.

	1	2	3
a)	cook	In the paper	have 2 years' experience
b)	truck driver	A friend told me about it	have a driver's license
c)	secretary	On a bulletin board	type 60 words per minute

	4	5
a)	$7 an hour	No
b)	$12 an hour	Yes, everything
c)	$400 per week	Health insurance

Terry: I'm interested in the job for a ______________________.
(1)

Gus: Where did you see it?

Terry: ______________________.
(2)

Gus: What are the qualifications?

Terry: You have to ______________________.
(3)

Gus: What is the salary?

Terry: ______________________.
(4)

Gus: Are there benefits?

Terry: ____________________ .
5

Gus: Are you going to apply?

Terry: Yes, I will fill out an application today.

B.

	1	2	3
a)	the factory	The pay is low	He's OK
b)	the donut shop	The work is boring	He's mean
c)	the hotel	I can't get a promotion	She doesn't care

	4	5
a)	fixing cars	mechanic
b)	accounting	bookkeeper
c)	preparing food	cook

Tim: How's your job at ____________________ ?
1

Jack: Not too good.

Tim: What's wrong?

Jack: ____________________ .
2

Tim: How's your boss?

Jack: ____________________ . I want to find a better job.
3

Tim: What are you interested in?

Jack: I have a lot of experience in ____________________ .
4

I think I'll try for a ____________________ .
5

Tim: Good luck.

C.

	1	2
a)	waiter	a restaurant
b)	manager	an apartment
c)	custodian	a company

Applicant: I'm calling about your ad in the paper.
Employer: Yes, it's still open. Are you currently employed?
Applicant: I'm a ____________ at ____________.
(1) (2)
Employer: Can you come in for an interview?
Applicant: This afternoon is fine with me.
Employer: Good. How about 2 o'clock?
Applicant: Fine, I'll see you then.

III. Reading

Caroline worked as a hotel clerk in her native country. She enjoyed her job. Then her family moved to the United States. She looked for a job, but she needed to learn English first. She went to an adult school. After a few months, one of her classmates told her about a job at a computer factory. She went there and asked about it. It was an assembly job. The salary was minimum wage and there were no benefits. The plant was very clean but it had very strong chemical smells and the work looked boring. She didn't take the job. "I will look for something better," she told her friend.

Exercise R-1: Try to use complete sentences.

1. What job did Caroline have in her native country?

   ____

2. Did she like her job there?

   ____

3. What did she need to learn when she came to the United States?

   ____

4. Who told her about the job at a computer factory?

   ____

5. What kind of job was it?

   ____

6. Why didn't she take the job?

   ____

IV. Structure

A. Review of Verbs in the Past Tense

Exercise S-1: Write the past tense form of these verbs.

Example: (clean) The gas station attendant <u>cleaned</u> the windows.

1. (cut) The butcher ______________ the meat yesterday.
2. (repair) ______________ the mechanic ______________ the car?
3. (take) The clerk ______________ inventory last week.
4. (not-file) Her secretary ______________ your report here.
5. (drive) That taxi driver ______________ to the station.
6. (mow) ______________ the gardener ______________ the lawn?
7. (not-clean) That custodian ______________ her office last night.
8. (use) The cashier ______________ the cash register.
9. (not-stock) The grocer ______________ the shelves.
10. (get) The employee ______________ there late.

Exercise: Answer the questions in the past tense. Use complete sentences.

1. What did you do yesterday?

   ____

2. What kind of work did you do in your native country?

   ____

3. What did you do the first day you came to the United States?

   ____

B. Future Verbs: Will

The future verb is for future action.

Examples: I will look for a job tomorrow.
They will start their work next week.

Verb: work

(will not = won't)

I will work	I won't work	Will I work?
You will work	You won't work	Will you work?
We will work	We won't work	Will we work?
They will work	They won't work	Will they work?
He will work	He won't work	Will he work?
She will work	She won't work	Will she work?
It will work	It won't work	Will it work?

C. Future Verbs: Contractions

Verb: come (will = 'll)

I will come = I'll come
You will come = You'll come
We will come = We'll come
They will come = They'll come
He will come = He'll come
She will come = She'll come
It will come = It'll come

Exercise S-2: Write the future of the verb.

Example: (fill) I will fill out the application tonight.

1. (take) The waitress ____________________ your order in a few minutes.
2. (make) The architects ____________________ the plans for the new building next month.
3. (fix) A plumber ____________________ your sink this afternoon.
4. (talk) We ____________________ to the union representative tomorrow.
5. (paint) Mr. Simpson, the house painter, ____________________ their home tomorrow.

Exercise S-3: Write the negative form of the future verb.

Example: (earn) He won't earn very much there.

1. (work) That police officer ________________ the night shift next week.
2. (give) Their employer ________________ them any benefits.
3. (go) I ________________ on vacation this year.
4. (apply) James ________________ for the new position.
5. (check) The accountant ________________ his books.

Exercise S-4: Write the question form of the future verb.

Example: (get) Will Clara get a better job?

1. (fill) __________ you __________ out the application?
2. (see) __________ your hairdresser __________ you today?
3. (change) __________ the boss __________ the schedule?
4. (deliver) __________ the florist __________ the flowers?
5. (report) __________ that journalist __________ on the peace talks?

Exercise S-5: Write the correct form of the future verb.

Example: (come) The carpenter will come to your home.

1. (talk) The manager ________________ to you tomorrow about the promotion.
2. (not-earn) He ________________ more at the new job.
3. (take) __________ the busboy __________ away those dirty dishes?
4. (deliver) The bus driver ________________ the packages to the store next week.

5. (write) ________ you ________ the lawyer a letter?
6. (call) I ________ my dentist tomorrow.
7. (not-be) The artist ________ here Saturday.
8. (work) The scientists ________ on a new project next year.
9. (get) ________ you ________ overtime at that job?
10. (not-ask) They ________ for a day off this weekend.

Exercise: Answer these questions. Use a complete sentence.

1. What will you do tomorrow?

   ____

2. Who will you visit soon?

   ____

3. When will you return to your native country?

   ____

4. Where will you go next month?

   ____

D. Too

Mary is studying English. James is studying English.
Mary is studying English and James is too.

Bob came to school. Gary came to school.
Bob came to school and Gary did too.

Rose works at the office. Tim works at the office.
Rose works at the office and Tim does too.

Martin will get his paycheck. Frank will get his paycheck.
Martin will get his paycheck and Frank will too.

Exercise S-6: Mark one sentence with too.

Example: I am here. Mary is here.
I am here and Mary is too.

1. Barbara is at home. Sandra is at home.
   Barbara is at home and Sandra ______________________.
2. I am going to work. My cousin is going to work.
   I am going to work and ______________________.
3. The package arrived. The letter arrived.
   ____
4. The carpenter came. The plumber came.
   ____
5. Martin will leave early. Jack will leave early.
   ____
6. You will stay there. My sister will stay there.
   ____
7. Sam works at the restaurant. Max works at the restaurant.
   ____
8. The TV was broken. The radio was broken.
   ____

Exercise:

I like ______________ and ______________ does too.

I will go to ______________ and ______________ will too.

I lived in ______________ and ______________ did too.

I am ______________ ing now and ______________ is too.

V. Writing

works Kim office an at

____

secretary She a is

____

She letters shorthand and types take

____

very Her is nice boss

____

from works Kim 8 A.M. 4 P.M. to

____

$2000 salary is month a her

____

She benefits has

____

Write

____

____

____

____

____

____

How about you, or a relative or friend?

____

____

____

____

____

____

VI. Pronunciation

long o ($\bar{o}$)

nose	boat	coat	toe
road	home	robe	toaster
smoke	hose	rose	blow
goat	soap	stove	rope
promotion	overtime	custodian	grocer
social security			

Listen:

1.________ 2.________ 3.________ 4.________ 5.________

6.________ 7.________ 8.________ 9.________ 10.________

VII. Life Skills

A. Finding a Job in the Want Ads

Want Ad Abbreviations:

co = company
exper = experience
hrs = hours
FT = full-time
cpl = couple
mgmt = management
mo = month
pref = preferred
refs = references
sal = salary
yr = year
DMV = Department of Motor Vehicles (driving record)
excel = excellent
gd = good
immed = immediately
even = evenings
med = medical
mgr = manager
nec = necessary
PT = part-time
S/H = shorthand
w = with
bnfts = benefits

HELP WANTED	HELP WANTED	HELP WANTED
DENTAL RECEPTIONIST, gd w phones, exper nec, FT, bnfts, 555-3206	COOK, dinner FT/PT, Call Rich at 555-9916	CASHIER, PT, Sat/Sun even, 6 pm—11 pm, will train, $5/hr, apply in person, 234 Elm St., San Ramon
MANAGEMENT, Sales, trainee, send resume to Mr. Dans, P.O. Box 32, Dawsonville	DRIVER, gd DMV, exper, 24 yrs+ pref, 555-3124	MANAGER, 12 unit apartment, cpl pref, 555-7392

Exercise L-1:

1. Which job ad tells the wage? ________
2. What jobs are part time? ________
3. The ________ and ________ jobs will train the person.
4. A couple is preferred for the ________ job.
5. Who do you call for the cook job? ________
6. A dental receptionist has to be good with ________.
7. Which job do you apply for in person? ________

8. Barry is 19 years old. He applied for the driver job but they preferred someone ______________________.

9. Which job has benefits? ______________________

10. How big is the apartment for the manager job? __________

B. Filling out a Social Security Application

SOCIAL SECURITY ADMINISTRATION
Application for a Social Security Card

Form Approved
OMB No. 0960-0066

INSTRUCTIONS

- Please read "How To Complete This Form" on page 2.
- Print or type using black or blue ink. DO NOT USE PENCIL.
- After you complete this form, take or mail it along with the required documents to your nearest Social Security office.
- If you are completing this form for someone else, answer the questions as they apply to that person. Then, sign your name in question 16.

1 NAME
To Be Shown On Card — FIRST / FULL MIDDLE NAME / LAST
FULL NAME AT BIRTH IF OTHER THAN ABOVE — FIRST / FULL MIDDLE NAME / LAST
OTHER NAMES USED

2 MAILING ADDRESS
Do Not Abbreviate — STREET ADDRESS, APT. NO., PO BOX, RURAL ROUTE NO.
CITY / STATE / ZIP CODE

3 CITIZENSHIP (Check One) — ☐ U.S. Citizen ☐ Legal Alien Allowed To Work ☐ Legal Alien Not Allowed To Work ☐ Foreign Student Allowed Restricted Employment ☐ Conditionally Legalized Alien Allowed To Work ☐ Other (See Instructions On Page 2)

4 SEX — ☐ Male ☐ Female

5 RACE/ETHNIC DESCRIPTION (Check One Only—Voluntary) — ☐ Asian, Asian-American Or Pacific Islander ☐ Hispanic ☐ Black (Not Hispanic) ☐ North American Indian Or Alaskan Native ☐ White (Not Hispanic)

6 DATE OF BIRTH — MONTH DAY YEAR

7 PLACE OF BIRTH (Do Not Abbreviate) — CITY / STATE OR FOREIGN COUNTRY — Office Use Only — FCI

8 MOTHER'S MAIDEN NAME — FIRST / FULL MIDDLE NAME / LAST NAME AT HER BIRTH

9 FATHER'S NAME — FIRST / FULL MIDDLE NAME / LAST

10 Has the person in item 1 ever received a Social Security number before?
☐ Yes (If "yes", answer questions 11-13.) ☐ No (If "no", go on to question 14.) ☐ Don't Know (If "don't know", go on to question 14.)

11 Enter the Social Security number previously assigned to the person listed in item 1.
☐☐☐-☐☐-☐☐☐☐

12 Enter the name shown on the most recent Social Security card issued for the person listed in item 1.
FIRST / MIDDLE / LAST

13 Enter any different date of birth if used on an earlier application for a card. MONTH / DAY / YEAR

14 TODAY'S DATE — MONTH DAY YEAR

15 DAYTIME PHONE NUMBER ( ) AREA CODE

DELIBERATELY FURNISHING (OR CAUSING TO BE FURNISHED) FALSE INFORMATION ON THIS APPLICATION IS A CRIME PUNISHABLE BY FINE OR IMPRISONMENT, OR BOTH.

16 YOUR SIGNATURE

17 YOUR RELATIONSHIP TO THE PERSON IN ITEM 1 IS: ☐ Self ☐ Natural Or Adoptive Parent ☐ Legal Guardian ☐ Other (Specify)

DO NOT WRITE BELOW THIS LINE (FOR SSA USE ONLY)

NPN		DOC	NTI	CAN		ITV	
PBC	EVI	EVA	EVC	PRA	NWR	DNR	UNIT

EVIDENCE SUBMITTED

SIGNATURE AND TITLE OF EMPLOYEE(S) REVIEWING EVIDENCE AND/OR CONDUCTING INTERVIEW

DATE

DCL — DATE

Form SS-5 (9/89) 5/88 edition may be used until supply is exhausted

C. Job Application

APPLICATION FOR WORK

Name Brown, Linda Date 5/15/91

Address 49 West St.

Hayward, CA 98786

Phone (415) 555-5674 Social Security # 570-89-9876

Job Desired Manager

Work Experience (Most recent work first)

Job	Address	Dates
Secretary	DFT Company, Salidan	1989-Now
Assembler	Wuz Electronics, Felton	1988-'89
Hotel Clerk	Ritz Hotel, Mexico City	1984-'87

Exercise L-2:

1. What job is Linda looking for? ____________
2. What job did she do outside the United States? ____________
3. What was her work for Wuz Electronics? ____________
4. What is her present job? ____________

How about you?

APPLICATION FOR WORK

Name ____________ Date ____________

Address ____________

____

Phone ____________ Social Security # ____________

Job Desired ____________

Work Experience (Most recent work first)

Job	Address	Dates

VIII. Critical Thinking

A.

B.

Vocabulary

outside
not happy
He needs a job.
He is holding a sign for a job.
They worked there before.
This person is asking for work.
These workers are on strike.
They don't like their working conditions.
signs
He is unemployed.
They are holding signs.

A. **B.**

1. ____________________
2. ____________________
3. ____________________

A.	B.
4. ____________________	4. ____________________
5. ____________________	5. ____________________
6. ____________________	6. ____________________
7. ____________________	7. ____________________

UNIT 11

TRANSPORTATION

How do you go from your home to school? Transportation is very necessary in our lives. We walk, drive, ride to many places. We use bikes, cars, buses, trains, planes, or just our feet. This unit is about how we use transportation.

Objectives

Competencies:

Traffic Signs
Bus Schedules

Structure

Future Verb: Going to
Helping Verbs: Must, Have to
Imperative
Either

Pronunciation:

(ow)

I. Vocabulary

A. Transportation

1. car/automobile/vehicle
2. van
3. truck
4. driver
5. passenger
6. bus
7. schedule
8. bus stop
9. bus station
10. bridge
11. toll booth
12. train
13. train station
14. ticket counter
15. railroad tracks
16. railroad crossing
17. street
18. road
19. highway
20. freeway
21. lane
22. divider
23. shoulder
24. curve
25. intersection
26. streetlight
27. signal
28. crosswalk
29. boat
30. ship
31. harbor
32. pier

B. Airport

1. ticket counter/check in
2. suitcase/luggage/ baggage
3. arrival
4. departure
5. security check
6. gate
7. ticket
8. boarding pass
9. terminal
10. baggage claim
11. customs
12. pilot
13. overhead compartment
14. carry-on luggage
15. window
16. aisle
17. flight attendant
18. runway
19. control tower

C. Parts of a Car

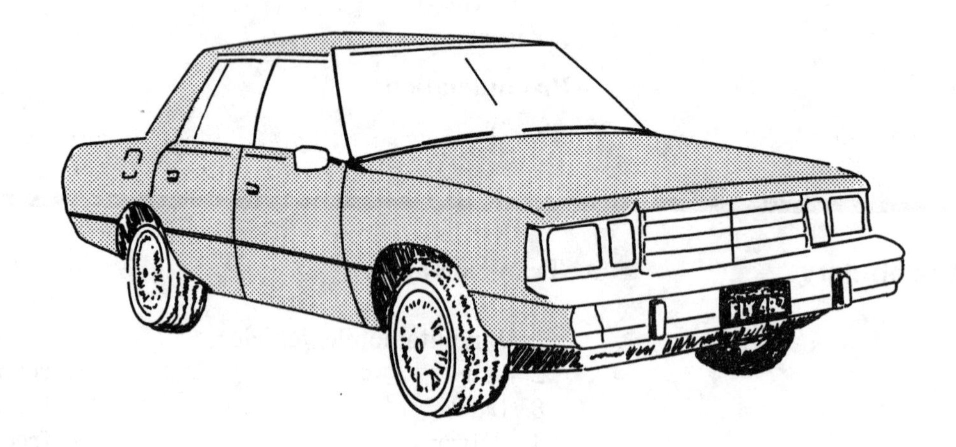

Outside

1. roof
2. trunk
3. rearview mirror
4. antenna
5. hood
6. headlights
7. grill
8. bumper
9. turn indicators
10. tires
11. hubcaps
12. wheels
13. door
14. doorhandle
15. side mirror
16. seats
17. seat belt
18. windshield
19. windshield wipers
20. fender

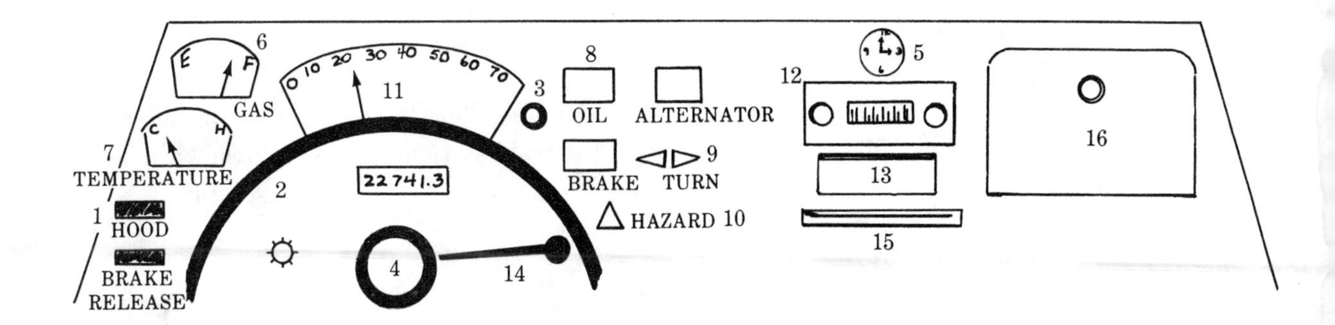

Inside

1. hood release
2. steering wheel
3. headlight control
4. horn
5. clock
6. fuel gauge
7. temperature gauge
8. oil gauge
9. turn signal
10. emergency lights
11. speedometer
12. radio
13. ashtray
14. gearshift
15. heater
16. glove compartment

II. Conversation

A.

	1	2	3
a)	The engine sounds bad	get a tune up	an oil change
b)	My tires are old	buy new ones	a tune up
c)	The battery's dead	recharge it	a smog check

Sal: I have a problem with my car.

Joe: What's the matter?

Sal: ______________________________ .
(1)

Joe: What are you going to do about it?

Sal: I'm going to ______________________________ .
(2)

Joe: My car has to have ____________________ (3). Where do you go?

Sal: John's Auto Repair is an honest place. It's on the corner of 4th Street and Trenton Avenue.

Joe: Thanks, I'll give it a try.

B.

	1	2
a)	Milliken Plaza	a few minutes
b)	the train station	a little while
c)	the airport	just a bit

Omar: I'm lost. How do you get to ______ (1) ?

Samira: Do you have a car?

Omar: No, I'm taking a bus.

Samira: Then take number 7. It comes on the hour.

Omar: Is there anything sooner?

Samira: Yes, number 8 will be here in ______ (2), but you have to make a transfer.

Omar: Oh, I'll take the 8. It's easier. Thanks a lot.

C.

	1	2
a)	bus	ride my bike
b)	train	walk

Carol: What kind of transportation do you like?

Peter: I have to take the ______ (1) to go to work. But on the weekends I like to ______ (2) .

Carol: I drive to work. There is always a lot of traffic. It's a headache.

Peter: And a lot of pollution too.

Carol: We need better public transportation.

Peter: I agree. I'm going to write a letter to my congressperson about it.

Carol: Me too.

III. Reading

Mrs. Martinez took the bus to work. It took her forty-five minutes to get there. Her friend told her, "Buy a car and it will take a short time and be more convenient." She took her advice. She decided to buy a car. She looked around at new cars but they were too expensive. The salesmen seemed very aggressive. Then she looked at used cars in the Want Ads of the newspaper. She found one and bought it.

She drove it to work everyday. She had to pay a lot for insurance and license registration. She got a tune up, an oil change and a smog check. Then one day the car got a flat tire. She didn't know how to change the tire. She called a mechanic and he told her that she needed new tires. She had to buy them. Not long after that she had an accident. It was not her fault but her car needed a lot of repair.

Finally she said to her friend, "This car is too much trouble for me. I'm going to sell this car and take the bus. It's a lot easier."

Exercise R-1: Answer the questions in complete sentences.

1. How long did it take for Mrs. Martinez to get to work by bus?

   ____

2. What did she decide to buy?

   ____

3. Why didn't she buy a new car?

   ____

4. Where did she find the used car?

   ____

5. Were the car insurance and license registration expensive?

   ____

6. Did the car need a tune up, oil change and smog check?

   ____

7. What happened when she had a flat tire?

   ____

8. What happened to her car in the accident?

   ____

9. What did she finally decide to do?

   ____

10. What is good about a car?

    ____

11. What is bad about a car?

    ____

IV. Structure

A. Future Verb: Going to

Another way to use the future is with going to.

Subject + verb be + going to + present verb

They're going to drive to school tomorrow.
He's going to take the bus next week.

Verb: do

I'm going to do	I'm not going to do	Am I going to do?
You're going to do	You aren't going to do	Are you going to do?
We're going to do	We aren't going to do	Are we going to do?
They're going to do	They aren't going to do	Are they going to do?
He's going to do	He isn't going to do	Is he going to do?
She's going to do	She isn't going to do	Is she going to do?
It's going to do	It isn't going to do	Is it going to do?

Exercise S-1: Write the future going to form.

Example: (take) I'm going to take the train.

1. (give) The policeman ______________________________ him a ticket for speeding.
2. (need) The car ______________________________ a tune up soon.
3. (put) The passengers ______________________________ their luggage in the overhead compartment.
4. (stop) The bus ______________________________ at the railroad crossing.
5. (buy) We ______________________________ our tickets at the ticket counter.

Exercise S-2: Write the negative form of going to.

Example: (fly) Sue isn't going to fly to Los Angeles next year.

1. (cross) The kids ______________________________ at the intersection.
2. (stay) The boat ______________________________ at that pier for a few days.
3. (change) They ______________________________ the oil.
4. (read) I ______________________________ the train schedule.
5. (drive) She ______________________________ on the freeway.

Exercise S-3: Write the question form of the future of going to.

Example: (try) Are they going to try another road?

1. (walk) ________ you ______________________ to work?
2. (tell) ________ the pilot ______________________ the passengers?
3. (stop) ________that car ______________________ at the crosswalk?
4. (ask) ________ Jack ______________________ for an aisle seat?
5. (check) ________ they ______________________ the departure time?

Exercise S-4: Write the going to future.

Example: (fix) The mechanic is going to fix your car tomorrow.

1. (drive) ________ you ______________________ to the terminal?
2. (take) I ______________________________ the train.
3. (not-get) He ______________________________ gas.
4. (pay) They ______________________________ at the tollbooth.
5. (go) ________ she ______________________ through customs?

6. (not-wash) Mr. Sen ______________________ his car today.
7. (pick) We ______________________ up a schedule next week.
8. (check) ________ your friends ________________ in?
9. (not-land) The plane ______________________ on another runway.
10. (park) The driver ______________________ his car on the shoulder of the road.

Exercise: Answer these future questions with complete sentences.

1. What are you going to do tomorrow?

   ____

2. What kind of transportation are you going to use?

   ____

3. Who are you going to talk to tonight?

   ____

4. What are you going to do next year?

   ____

B. Helping Verb: Must, Have to

Must or have to is used for a strong recommendation or necessity.

They must get there on time or they will lose their jobs.
The man is very sick. You must call an ambulance.
It's late. He has to pick up his children.
The students have to pass their driving exams.

Exercise S-5: Use must in these sentences.

1. He ______________ renew his license every year.
2. They ______________ use their seat belts.
3. Kim ______________ take the final exam.

Use have to or has to in these sentences.

4. I ________________ leave now.
5. The passenger ________________ buy his ticket.
6. Does Helen ________________ get there early?

Negative:

He must not arrive late.
She doesn't have to take the driving test.

Exercise S-6: Use must or have to in your answer.

Example: He has a doctor's appointment at 5. He must go now.
or He has to leave now.

1. She has a test tomorrow. She ________________ study.
2. Their car has a flat tire. They ________________ fix it.
3. He doesn't know the bus schedule. He ________________ read it.

C. Imperative

The imperative of the verb is for a command or request. You don't write the subject you. It can be singular or plural.

Sit down please.
Come here.
Turn right at the intersection.

The negative of the imperative is don't plus the present verb.

Don't open that door.
Don't take this bus.

Exercise S-7: Write the imperative form.

Example: (stop) Stop here please.

1. (exit) ________________ on the left.
2. (not-write) ________________ below that line.
3. (close) ________________ that door please.
4. (not-go) ________________ . It's too early.

5. (not-take) ______________ the 8 bus. (take) ______________ the 9.
6. (come) Please ______________ in.

People use the imperative to give directions.

Go down Idaho Street and then turn left on Poplar Avenue. Go about seven blocks. Pass the high school and turn right on Baldwin Street. It's on your right, number 560 Baldwin.

What are the directions to where you live?

____

____

____

An imperative with the speaker uses let us or Let's. Let's is more popular.

Let's go now.
Let's leave.
Let's not drive there.

Exercise S-8: Use the speaker imperative.

Example: (take) Let's take this bus.

1. (call) ______________ the mechanic.
2. (check) ______________ our baggage.
3. (not-sit) ______________ in the smoking section.
4. (do) ______________ something about pollution.

What about now? Let's ______________________.

D. Either

The truck isn't here. Their car isn't here.
The truck isn't here and their car isn't either.

I'm not working. The mechanic isn't working.
I'm not working and the mechanic isn't either.

The bus doesn't go there. The train doesn't go there.
The bus doesn't go there and the train doesn't either.

She didn't drive to work. He didn't drive to work.
She didn't drive to work and he didn't either.

Sara won't come. Mary won't come.
Sara won't come and Mary won't either.

You aren't going to take the plane. They aren't going to take the plane.
You aren't going to take the plane and they aren't either.

Exercise S-9: Make one sentence with either.

Example: I'm not here. Gail isn't here.
I'm not here and Gail isn't either.

1. Sam isn't on the bus. Frank isn't on the bus.

   Sam isn't on the bus and ______________________.

2. We aren't talking. The bus driver isn't talking.

   ______________________________.

3. The cable car doesn't go downtown. The train doesn't go downtown.

   ______________________________.

4. The boat didn't leave. The yacht didn't leave.

   ____

5. I won't drive over the speed limit. He won't drive over the speed limit.

   ______________________________.

6. Val isn't going to take a vacation. Gilbert isn't going to take a vacation.

   ____

Exercise:

I don't like ______________ and ______________ doesn't either.

I won't go to ______________ and ______________ won't either.

I didn't live in ______________ and ______________ didn't either.

I'm not going to ______________ and ______________ isn't either.

I'm not ______________ ing now and ______________ isn't either.

V. Writing

takes Luis bus school to the

____

8:00 bus stop He at waits the at

____

at The comes 8:10 bus

____

crowded always It is

____

He his friend the meets on bus

____

the 8:40 They off bus get at

____

They school at 8:50 at arrive

____

School 9:00 at starts

____

Write:

____

____

____

____

____

____

____

How about you?

____

____

____

____

____

____

____

VI. Pronunciation

ow

found	cow	hour	brown
down	about	cloud	shout
pound	crowd	ground	noun
town	how	now	mouse

Listen:

1.________ 2.________ 3.________ 4.________ 5.________

6.________ 7.________ 8.________ 9.________ 10.________

VII. Life Skills

A. Traffic Signs

DO NOT
ENTER
a.

b.

c.

d.

e.

NO
TURN
ON RED
f.

g.

SPEED
LIMIT
50
h.

Exercise L-1: Match the sign to the sentence.

1. Come to a full stop. ________
2. Don't turn here at red signal. ________
3. The traffic goes in only one direction. ________
4. Don't go over 50 miles per hour. ________
5. Don't enter here. ________
6. Let the other cars go first. ________
7. Don't make a turn to go in the opposite direction. ________
8. Drive carefully. Children are walking near here. ________

Exercise L-2: Circle the right answer.

1. a. no turns
   b. left turn only
   c. no left turn

2. a. signal ahead
   b. train crossing
   c. intersection

3. a. curvy road
   b. bumpy road
   c. straight road

4. a. flooded road
   b. slippery
   c. closed

B. Bus Schedule

DAILY SERVICE: Sunnyvale—Pleasanton

Departing	Time	Arriving	Time
Sunnyvale	6:00 A.M.	Pleasanton	8:00 A.M.
Pleasanton	8:30 A.M.	Sunnyvale	10:30 A.M.
Sunnyvale	11:00 A.M.	Pleasanton	1:00 P.M.
Pleasanton	1:30 P.M.	Sunnyvale	3:30 P.M.
Sunnyvale	4:00 P.M.	Pleasanton	6:00 P.M.

One Way $8.00 / Round Trip $15.00

Exercise L-3:

1. What time is the first bus to Pleasanton? ____________
2. How long is the trip from Sunnyvale to Pleasanton? ____________

3. Clyde lives in Sunnyvale. He wants to go to Pleasanton to visit his grandmother in the morning.

   What time should he take the bus? ______________

   How much will his round trip ticket be? ______________

4. Ruth lives in Pleasanton. She is going to have dinner with her friend in Sunnyvale at 5:30 and stay overnight.

   At what time should she take the bus? ______________

BUS STOP
57

Oak to Main Street
via
7th Avenue

Service:
7 A.M.—11 P.M.
Every 15 minutes

Exercise L-4:

1. What is the number of the bus? ______________
2. Where does it begin? ______________
3. Where does it end? ______________
4. Does the bus go along 7th Avenue? ______________
5. How often does the bus come? ______________
6. Can John get this bus at 1:00 in the morning? ______________

VIII. Critical Thinking

A.

B.

Vocabulary

transportation
freeway
commuters
The freeway is crowded.
They are getting on and off the train
The train is stopping for passengers.

car pollution
train station
public transportation
They are going somewhere.
The cars are moving slowly.

A.

1. ____________________
2. ____________________
3. ____________________
4. ____________________
5. ____________________
6. ____________________
____
7. ____________________
____

B.

4. ____________________
5. ____________________
6. ____________________
____
7. ____________________
____

Is car pollution a problem? ____________________

____

____

____

UNIT 12

COMMUNICATION

People in the world communicate by many different ways. We talk to each other, speak on the phone, write letters, and enjoy entertainment. This unit is about the importance of communication in a world that is getting smaller.

Objectives

Competencies:

Telephone Listings and Rates
Addressing an Envelope and Writing a Letter
Art and Entertainment Listings

Structure

Verb, Noun, Pronoun, Adjective, and Preposition Review

Pronunciation:

(aw)
Review

I. Vocabulary

A. Telephone

1. receiver
2. cord/cordless
3. receiver button
4. hook
5. dial
   rotary/touchtone
6. dial tone
7. number
8. area code
9. directory/phone book
10. listing
11. white pages
12. yellow pages
13. phone booth/public phone
14. coin/slot
15. call/make a call/phone
16. answering machine
17. wrong number
18. rates
19. fax

B. Post Office

1. mailbox
2. letter
3. envelope
4. send/mail
5. postal clerk
6. letter carrier/mailman/
   mailwoman
7. stamp
8. postage
9. return address
10. forward
11. express mail
12. airmail
13. special delivery
14. first class
15. insured mail
16. registered mail
17. package
18. postmark

C. Entertainment and Arts

1. museum
2. art gallery
3. zoo
4. county fair
5. night club
6. show
7. theater
8. musical
9. play/drama
10. concert
11. music
    - classical
    - popular
    - rock
    - country
12. television/TV
13. movie:
    - romance
    - comedy
    - mystery
    - western
    - action/adventure
    - documentary
14. video
15. cassette

II. Conversation

A.

Kris:	Do you use the phone much?
Jim:	I usually prefer to talk to people in person.
Kris:	Me too. But the phone is very convenient. I call my parents long distance every week.
Jim:	It's good for finding information, too. I use the directory all the time. The yellow pages have all the kinds of businesses you can use.
Kris:	The only thing I don't like are sales calls.
Jim:	And when someone has the wrong number.
Kris:	We are going to get an answering machine next week. When we are not at home, it can take messages.
Jim:	Sounds good. Well, I have to run now. See you later.

B.

	1	2
a)	send a package	stamps
b)	check my post office box	big envelopes
c)	mail an express letter	postcards

Ron: Where are you going?

Natalie: To the post office. I need to ________________.
(1)

Ron:	Could you buy some ________ (2) for me while you're there?
Natalie:	Sure, I don't mind.
Ron:	Did the mail come yet?
Natalie:	No, I don't think the carrier passed by. She usually comes at noon.
Ron:	I'm expecting an important letter. I hope it gets here today.

C.

	1	2	3	4
a)	comedy	drama	museum	art
b)	westerns	adventure	concert	music
c)	mysteries	documentaries	theater	drama

Chu:	What do you like to do on the weekend?
Yoshiko:	Different things. Usually I like to go outside, like to a zoo or park. At night I like to rent a video movie.
Chu:	What kind of movies do you like?
Yoshiko:	________ (1). What about you?
Chu:	I prefer a movie theater. I enjoy ________ (2). But on the weekends I like to go to a ________ (3).
Yoshiko:	Really?
Chu:	Yes, ________ (4) is very interesting for me. I studied it in school.

III. Reading

In the morning Samira tried to call her friend, Naser, but he wasn't home. She left a message on his answering machine. She had free tickets to a musical at the local concert hall and wanted to invite him. Her brother was a performer in it. He was a good singer. She was very proud of him. The show was about world peace. It started at 8 P.M.

About two hours later Naser returned the call. He said, "I had to go to the post office. I sent a package to my niece. Thanks for the invitation to the show tonight. I can go. I really like musicals."

Samira answered, "I went to the post office, too. I had to mail an express letter to my uncle in Dallas. I'm glad you can come. My sister and I will pick you up at 7:30."

Exercise R-1: Answer the questions.

1. Why didn't Naser answer the phone when Samira called?

   ____

2. What did Samira want to tell him?

   ____

3. How did Naser get the message?

   ____

4. What was the theme of the musical?

   ____

5. Who was Samira proud of? Why?

   ____

6. What did Samira's brother do in the musical?

   ____

7. Did Naser agree to go to the show?

   ____

8. When did Samira and her sister plan to pick Naser up?

   ____

IV. Structure

A. Verb Review

Exercise S-1: Underline the verbs in this paragraph. Write them below and explain what tense each one is.

> Karen is planning now for her trip to the city tomorrow. She will visit the art and history museums. She loves paintings and history. Her mother is a painter and her uncle teaches world history at the local college.
>
> Last week she went to the zoo with her friends. They had a great time. The weather was nice and the animals were very interesting. She took a lot of pictures.

		Verb	Tense
Example:	1.	is planning	present continuous
	2.		
	3.		
	4.		
	5.		
	6.		
	7.		
	8.		
	9.		
	10.		

Exercise S-2: Write the correct form of the verb with the indicated tense.

Example: (write-present continuous) He is writing a letter now.

1. (call-present) He ________________ his mother every month.
2. (send-past) They ________________ the package last year.
3. (perform-future) The singers ________________ in Los Angeles next week.
4. (write-present continuous) I ________________ a letter to my friend right now.
5. (deliver-past) ________ the mail carrier ________________ the mail at noon yesterday?
6. (put-present) ________ you always ________________ your return address on the envelope?
7. (insure-future) ________ your brother ________________ the package?
8. (dial-present continuous) ________ Sharon ________________ now?
9. (be-past) ________ it the wrong number?
10. (not-look-future) Harold and Maude ________________ at TV tonight.

11. (not-forward-past) The post office ______________________ the letter.

12. (not-answer-present) Rose ______________________ the phone.

13. (not-rent-present continuous) We ______________________ any videos now.

14. (not-be-present) Mark ______________________ here.

Exercise S-3: Write the correct form of the verb.

Example: (talk) He is talking on the phone now.

1. (send) She ______________ the express mail yesterday.
2. (go) They ______________ to the concert tomorrow.
3. (look) I ______________ in the yellow pages now.
4. (find) ______________ he ______________ the area code last week?
5. (drive) Everyday Mrs. Hart ______________ to the mail box.
6. (not-leave) Frank ______________ the receiver off the hook last night.
7. (play) ______________ your children ______________ in the park tomorrow?
8. (listen) ______________ you ______________ to the radio every day?
9. (act) He ______________ in the play next week.
10. (watch) ______________ your sister ______________ TV now?
11. (not-pay) I ______________ that much money for the movie tomorrow.
12. (not-like) They ______________ classical music.
13. (go) ______________ you ______________ to the game tomorrow?
14. (be) The students ______________ in class yesterday.
15. (not-do) Tien ______________ anything important now.

Exercise: Answer these questions with complete sentences.

1. What are you doing now?

   ____

2. What did you do yesterday?

   ____

3. What will you do tomorrow?

   ____

4. What are you going to do next week?

   ____

5. What do you do every day?

   ____

Helping Verb Review: <u>Can</u>, <u>Should</u>, <u>Must</u>, <u>Have to</u>

Exercise S-4: Write <u>can</u>, <u>should</u>, <u>must</u> or <u>have to</u> in the spaces.

Example: They have an exam tomorrow. They <u>must</u> study.

1. There is a good movie at the theater. You ______________ go and see it.
2. Isn't that wonderful? He ______________ speak three languages.
3. Jan is very sick. She ______________ go to the doctor.
4. You ______________ visit the museum when you're here.
5. Bob doesn't work tomorrow. He ______________ come to your party.

Exercise: Write your own sentences.

I can ____.

I should ____.

I must ____.

I have to ____.

B. Nouns

Exercise S-5: Write the plurals of these nouns.

Example: letter letters

1. phone ____________________
2. directory ____________________
3. pass ____________________
4. play ____________________
5. child ____________________
6. watch ____________________
7. tooth ____________________
8. life ____________________
9. woman ____________________
10. library ____________________

Exercise S-6: Write much or many in the spaces.

Example: How many calls did you make?

1. How ________________ stamps do you need?
2. How ________________ postage was on the letter?
3. There is too ________________ water in the pool.
4. There are ________________ tickets available.
5. He has too ________________ money.

Exercise S-7: Write little or few in the spaces.

Example: There were a few seats available.

1. I have very ________________ mail.
2. They saw ________________ students there.
3. The musician played a ________________ songs.
4. She has a ________________ money.
5. There is ________________ time remaining.

Exercise S-8: Write the possessive.

Example: the guitar of Maria
Maria's guitar

1. the pen of John

____

2. the letters of Kathy

____

3. the rates of the telephone companies

____

4. I saw the truck of the mail carrier.

____

5. Mary likes the paintings of the museums.

____

C. Pronouns

Exercise S-9: Choose the correct pronoun.

Example: (he/him) I like him.

1. (I/me) They are looking at ______________ .
2. (She/Her) ______________ is here.
3. (they/them) How much did ______________ spend?
4. (we/us) He told ______________ the answer.
5. (my/mine) That is ______________ book.
6. (their/theirs) Those are our seats and those are ______________ .
7. (myself/yourself) Did you hurt ______________ ?
8. (himself/themselves) He studies by ______________ .
9. (some/any) He didn't have ______________ extra change.
10. (some/any) She delivered ______________ letters.

D. Adjectives

Exercise S-10: Write the opposites of these adjectives.

Example: bad <u>good</u>

1. old ________________
2. correct ________________
3. fast ________________
4. dirty ________________
5. hot ________________
6. rich ________________
7. fat ________________
8. noisy ________________
9. easy ________________
10. soft ________________
11. He's ________________, not short.
12. The store is ________________, not closed.

Exercise S-11: Write the comparative or superlative of these adjectives.

Examples: (fast) Express mail is <u>faster</u> than airmail.
(expensive) The call to New York was the <u>most expensive</u>.

1. (tall) He is ________________ than you.
2. (busy) Christmas is the ________________ day of the year for the phone company.
3. (beautiful) The painting is ________________ than that statue.
4. (big) Mexico is ________________ than Costa Rica.
5. (difficult) Mathematics is the ________________ of his five subjects at school.
6. (good) The restaurant has the ________________ pizza in the city.
7. (bad) The news was ________________ than a horror movie.

Exercise: Answer these questions with complete sentences.

What kind of music is the best?

____

Which kind of food is the most delicious?

____

Who is more patient, your mother or your father?

____

What is larger, where you live now or where you lived before?

____

E. Prepositions

Exercise S-12: Write the correct proposition in, on, at, between, under, with, for.

Example: His wallet is in his pocket.

1. The stamp is ______________ the envelope.
2. I went to the movie ______________ John.
3. The gift is ______________ you.
4. Chicago is ______________ the State of Illinois.
5. The apartment is ______________ the two houses.
6. He hides the key ______________ the doormat.
7. He's going to the park ______________ Tuesday ______________ the morning.
8. ______________ 3 o'clock the boat will go ______________ the bridge.

V. Writing

went city I last the to week

____

museum visited a I science

____

It interesting very was

____

best I about liked the exhibit astronomy the

____

astronaut want I be to an

____

future in Maybe live space will the in we

____

later See you

____

Write

Dear Jonathan:

____

____

____

____

____

Sincerely,
Dwight

How about you?

Dear ________________:

____

____

____

____

____

Sincerely,

____

VI. Pronunciation

aw

saw	thought	caught	taught
ball	hall	long	dog
cough	wrong	talk	boss
lost	walk	cost	call

Listen:

1.________ 2.________ 3.________ 4.________ 5.________

6.________ 7.________ 8.________ 9.________ 10.________

Review

address	plate	bell	key
bill	eye	nut	wanted
coughed	played	huge	clock
road	mouse	lamp	native
letter	between	children	child
truck	tool	rob	nose
crowd			

Listen:

1.________ 2.________ 3.________ 4.________ 5.________

6.________ 7.________ 8.________ 9.________ 10.________

11.________12.________

VII. Life Skills

A. Phone Listings and Rates

CITY OF MILTON DIRECTORY

DAVID'S RESTAURANT 134 Main St 555-8695
Davidson Howard 59 Club Dr 555-8320
Davidson Lucy Mrs. 21 Martinez Rd 555-3423
Davies A 555-2132
DAVIES APPLIANCES 118 Dundee Dr 555-8734
Davis Berle Dance Arts Center 3321 Brittan Ave 555-9812
Davis Arnold 21341 Harding St 555-8967

Exercise L-1: Answer the questions about the above listings.

1. What street does Howard Davidson live on? ________________
2. What is David's Restaurant's phone number? ________________
3. What is Arnold Davis' phone number? ________________
4. The phone number for Lucy Davidson is ________________.
5. Where does A. Davis live? ________________
6. Nick wants to buy a refrigerator. What number can he call?

   ____

7. Mrs. Hart's daughter wants to learn ballet. What number should she call for information? ________________

TIME	WEEKDAYS (including holiday eves.)	HOLIDAYS (including Thanksgiving)	SATURDAYS (including Christmas Day and New Years Day this year)	SUNDAYS
8 am to 5 pm	Regular Rates	Save 40% to other states ——— Save 60% within California	Save 60%	Save 60%
5 pm to 11 pm	Save 40% to other states ——— Save 30% within California		Save 60%	Save 40% to other states ——— Save 60% within California
11 pm to 8 am	Save 60%	Save 60%	Save 60%	Save 60%

NOTE: 40% and 60% discounts apply in the 48 continental states;
30% and 55% in Alaska and Hawaii.

Exercise L-2: Answer the questions.

1. What are the times on a week day when you can save 60% on your phone calls? ________________
2. When are regular rates? ________________
3. Bruce wants to call his friend in another state on the 4th of July. When is the cheapest time to call him? ________________

B. Writing a Letter and Addressing an Envelope

John Adams
64 Broadway
Palmer, Utah 84403

25 USA

Mr. John Doe
8181 State Street
Centerville, Ohio 43081

You went to a concert of the popular singer Joe Sartori. He gave all the money from the concert to help starving people in the world. You think this was a good idea. Write a letter to him and address the envelope with your return address. His address is: Joe Sartori, 6198 Ralston Ave., San Mateo, California 94401.

STAMP

Dear ________________,

____

____

____

____

____

____

____

____

C. Entertainment Page

EVENTS

Circus, Downtown Arena, Sat and Sun 2 and 7:30 P.M.

Flower Exhibition, Hall of Flowers, Kennedy Park, June 13th-18th, 10 AM-4 PM

Shakespeare's Romeo and Juliet, Belmont Theater, Fri, Sat and Sun at 8 PM

CONCERTS

Classical-Beethoven 5th Symphony City Orchestra, Ariel Hall, Sat 8 PM

Rock—The Bad Boys, Colliseum, Fri and Sat 8 PM

Musical—"Les Miserables" University Theater, Fri and Sat at 8 PM, Sun at 2 PM

FREE Concert, The City Band, Central Park, Sun at 1 PM

Exercise L-3: Answer the questions.

1. What are the times of the circus performances?

   ____

2. Where will the flower exhibition take place?

   ____

3. What is the name of the rock group playing at the Colliseum?

   ____

4. What kind of music is the city orchestra playing on Saturday?

   ____

5. Enrique doesn't work Saturday. When can he see Romeo and Juliet?

   ____

6. When can the Martin family see the flower exhibition?

____

7. Karen wants to go to see "Les Miserables" but it's sold out on Friday and Saturday. When can she go?

____

8. Steve has very little money. Where can he go to listen to music?

____

VIII. Critical Thinking

Vocabulary

mural	outside
inside	painting
wall	realism
museum	abstract

She is looking at a painting.
They are recognizing the pictures in the mural.
She is thinking about the meaning of the painting.
They are looking at the mural.

A.

B.

A.	B.
1. ______	1. ______
2. ______	2. ______
3. ______	3. ______
4. ______	4. ______
5. ______ ______	5. ______ ______
6. ______ ______	6. ______ ______

What kind of art do you like?

____

____

____

____

Appendix

1. Print Letters
2. Cursive Letters
3. Temperature C°/F°
4. Measurements
5. Irregular Verbs

Please Write (the alphabet in small letters)

Please Write (the alphabet in capitol letters)

Cursive Writing

Aa Bb Cc Dd Ee

Ff Gg Hh Ii Jj

Kk Ll Mm Nn

Oo Pp Qq Rr Ss

Tt Uu Vv Ww Xx

Yy Zz

A a

Upper case
Capital letter

Lower case
Small letter

stroke

* NOTE: If you have problems using the cursive writing, practice the alphabet in your house and follow the strokes given to you in this lesson. Practice as many times as you need. You must be able to write with print writing as well as with cursive writing.

THE ENGLISH ALPHABET

➤ **Print Writing**

Capital Letters

A B C D E F G H I J K L M N O P Q R S T U V W X Y Z

Small Letters

a b c d e f g h i j k l m n o p q r s t u v w x y z

Capital Letters

➤ **Cursive Writing**

A B C D E F G H I J K L M N O P Q

R S T U V W X Y Z

Small Letters

a b c d e f g h i j k l m n o p q

r s t u v w x y z

➤ **Arabic Numbers**

1 2 3 4 5 6 7 8 9 10

➤ **Roman Numbers**

I II III IV V VI VII VIII IX X

Punctuation

➤ **Symbols**

!	?	&	%	$	¢
Exclamation Point	**Question Mark**	**And**	**Percent**	**Money**	**Cents**

➤ **Marks**

.	,	:	;	“ ”
Period	**Comma**	**Semi-Colon**	**Colon**	**Quotation Marks**

Temperature C/F

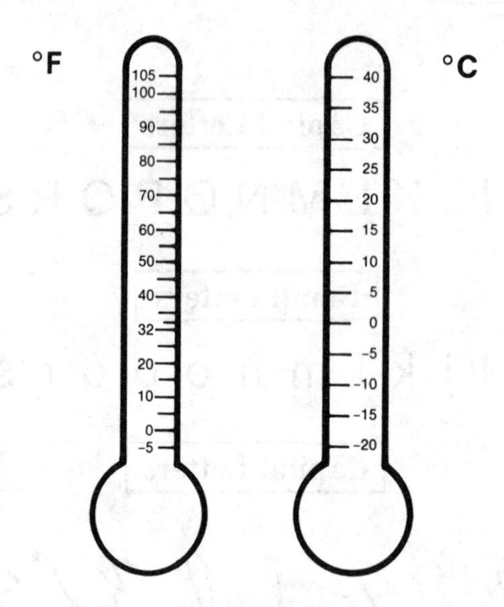

Metric Conversion Factors (Approximate)

Conversions TO Metric Measures

	Symbol	When You Know	Multiply By	To Find	Symbol
LENGTH	in	inches	2.5	centimeters	cm
	ft	feet	30	centimeters	cm
	yd	yards	0.9	meters	m
	mi	miles	1.6	kilometers	km
MASS (weight)	oz	ounces	28	grams	g
	lb	pounds	0.45	kilograms	kg
VOLUME	tsp	teaspoons	5	milliliters	ml
	Tbsp	tablespoons	15	milliliters	ml
	fl oz	fluid ounces	30	milliliters	ml
	c	cups	0.24	liters	l
	pt	pints	0.47	liters	l
	qt	quarts	0.95	liters	l
	gal	gallons	3.8	liters	l
TEMP. $C = \frac{5}{9}(F - 32)$	°F	Fahrenheit temperature	5/9 (after subtracting 32)	Celsius temperature	°C

°F: -40, 0, 32, 40, 80, 98.6, 120, 160, 200, 212 °F

°C: -40, -20, 0, 20, 37, 40, 60, 80, 100 °C

Irregular Verbs

Base	Past	Past Participle
awake	awoke (less commonly, *awaked*)	awaked, awoken
be	was	been
bear	bore	born (birthdate) borne (carried)
beat	beat	beaten
begin	began	begun
bend	bent	bent
bet	bet	bet
bite	bit	bitten
bleed	bled	bled
blow	blew	blown
break	broke	broken
bring	brought	brought
broadcast	broadcast, broadcasted	broadcast, broadcasted
build	built	built
burst	burst	burst
buy	bought	bought
cast	cast	cast
catch	caught	caught
choose	chose	chosen
come	came	come
cost	cost	cost
cut	cut	cut
deal	dealt	dealt
dig	dug	dug
dive	dived, dove	dived
do	did	done
draw	drew	drawn
dream	dreamed, dreamt	dreamed, dreamt
drink	drank	drunk
drive	drove	driven
eat	ate	eaten
fall	fell	fallen
feed	fed	fed
feel	felt	felt
fight	fought	fought
find	found	found
flee	fled	fled
fly	flew	flown
forbid	forbade	forbidden
forget	forgot	forgotten
forgive	forgave	forgiven
freeze	froze	frozen
get	got	got, gotten
give	gave	given

Irregular Verbs

Base	Past	Past Participle
go	went	gone
grind	ground	ground
grow	grew	grown
hang	hung, hanged	hung, hanged
have	had	had
hear	heard	heard
hide	hid	hidden
hit	hit	hit
hold	held	held
hurt	hurt	hurt
keep	kept	kept
kneel	kneeled, knelt	kneeled, knelt
knit	knitted, knit	knitted, knit
know	knew	known
lay	laid	laid
lead	led	led
leap	leaped, leapt	leaped, leapt
leave	left	left
lend	lent	lent
let	let	let
lie	lay	lain
light	lighted, lit	lighted, lit
lose	lost	lost
make	made	made
mean	meant	meant
meet	met	met
overcome	overcame	overcome
pay	paid	paid
put	put	put
read	read	read
ride	rode	ridden
ring	rang	rung
rise	rose	risen
run	ran	run
say	said	said
see	saw	seen
sell	sold	sold
sent	sent	sent
set	set	set
sew	sewed	sewn
shake	shook	shaken
shine	shone, shined	shone, shined
shoot	shot	shot
show	showed	shown, showed
shrink	shrank, shrunk	shrunk

shut	shut	shut
sing	sang	sung
sink	sank, sunk	sunk
sit	sat	sat
sleep	slept	slept
slide	slid	slid
speak	spoke	spoken
speed	speeded, sped	speeded, sped
spend	spent	spent
spin	spun	spun
spit	spit, spat	spit, spat
split	split	split
spread	spread	spread
spring	sprang, sprung	sprung
stand	stood	stood
steal	stole	stolen
stick	stuck	stuck
sting	stung	stung
strike	struck	struck
swear	sworn	sworn
sweep	swept	swept
swim	swam	swum
swing	swung	swung
take	took	taken
teach	taught	taught
tear	tore	torn
tell	told	told
think	thought	thought
throw	threw	thrown
understand	understood	understood
wake	woke, waked	waked, woken
wear	wore	worn
weave	wove	woven
weep	wept	wept
win	won	won
withdraw	withdrew	withdrawn
withhold	withheld	withheld
wring	wrung	wrung
write	wrote	written

Answer Key

Introduction

These introductory exercises have been designed for students to practice identifying and writing letters. The teacher can bring real signs into the classroom or even take the class for a walk around outside, finding signs and letters. The exercises labeled "Look" are writing or identifying exercises and can be done individually, in pairs or small groups, or with the whole class. The exercises marked "Listen" are intended for the teacher to read, and the student to listen and mark the correct answer.

Look (Students will match capital letter to small letter.)

1. a
2. n
3. j
4. b
5. e
6. x
7. u
8. h
9. p
10. r
11. d
12. l
13. k
14. q
15. z
16. t
17. c
18. f
19. w
20. y
21. g
22. s
23. v
24. o
25. m
26. i

Listen (Teacher will read each letter aloud, and student will circle correct letter.)

1. p
2. t
3. H
4. e
5. z
6. W
7. b
8. g
9. N
10. s
11. y
12. u
13. R
14. L
15. f
16. c
17. I
18. m
19. v
20. O
21. j
22. A
23. d
24. K
25. q
26. x

Listen (Teacher spells out and pronounces each word; students fill in missing letters.)

1. name
2. Robert
3. city
4. address
5. Mr. Carson
6. telephone
7. Mary Brown
8. first
9. last
10. country
11. age
12. jail
13. Mrs. Davidson
14. walk
15. zip
16. box
17. quick

Puzzle

L	A	S	T	I	E	C	O	U	N	T	R	Y	G	H
D	G	V	X	W	G	M	I	G	A	F	I	R	S	T
Y	E	Y	O	U	K	T	W	Q	M	W	P	U	I	D
A	N	F	B	N	S	C	Z	M	E	Y	I	L	B	L
D	A	T	E	O	F	B	I	R	T	H	N	C	T	A
Z	G	Z	S	W	T	U	V	R	I	N	C	F	X	N
I	N	A	T	I	O	N	A	L	I	T	Y	E	A	G
P	S	P	B	X	N	T	O	R	F	G	L	M	G	U
C	S	V	N	S	J	D	M	A	L	E	F	A	E	A
O	B	I	R	T	H	P	L	A	C	E	N	L	Y	G
D	A	D	D	R	E	S	S	C	V	R	I	E	E	E
E	F	E	M	A	T	E	L	E	P	H	O	N	E	B

In the last exercise in the introduction, the teacher and students can work together to identify words and numbers relevant to their lives.

UNIT 1—Identification

Only a partial list of countries and nationalities is given, but the main suffixes are there. The teacher and students can write in the countries of students not found in the unit.

III. Reading

Ex. R-1:

1. student
2. Brett
3. David
4. native country
5. French
6. Middletown
7. address
8. apartment
9. apartment number
10. 555-9821
11. Paris, France

IV. Structure

Ex. S-1:

1. am
2. are
3. is
4. are
5. are
6. is
7. is
8. are
9. is
10. is

Ex. S-2:

1. b
2. a
3. c
4. b
5. c
6. a

Ex. S-3:

1. is
2. is
3. are
4. is
5. are

Ex. S-4:

1. he's
2. I'm
3. it's
4. they're
5. she's
6. you're
7. we're

Ex. S-5:

books, pencils, pens, states, languages, notebooks, eraser, name, number

Ex. S-6:

1. are
2. is
3. are
4. is
5. is

V. Writing

Ex. W-1:

They are students.
You come from Italy.
It is a registration form.
He is Japanese.
We're nice people.

VII. Lifeskills

Ex. L-1:

1. His first name is James.
2. His last name is Cool.
3. His address is 1516 Elm St., San Mateo, CA 94401.
4. His license number is J7891650.

Ex. L-2:

1. Her first name is Mary.
2. Her last name is Hart.
3. His address is 747 Elm St., San Mateo, CA 94401.
4. His license number is J7891650.
5. Her phone number is (415) 375-4797.

VIII. Critical Thinking

A.	B.
1. woman	1. man
2. office	2. class
3. work	3. study
4. job	4. book
5. answer phone	5. school
6. She is a worker.	6. He is a student.
7. She is at work.	7. He is in class.

UNIT 2—Time

I. Vocabulary

Ex. V-1:

1. hot
2. cool
3. warm
4. cold
5. warm

Ex. V-2:

1. thirty-eight
2. forty-three
3. eighty-four
4. fifty-two
5. ninety-five
6. sixty-seven
7. ninety-nine
8. thirty-one
9. seventy-six
10. forty-four

Ex. V-3:

1. 96
2. 77
3. 51
4. 48
5. 62
6. 84
7. 33
8. 92
9. 39
10. 66

Ex. V-4 and V-5: (Teacher can dictate from vocabulary words given in D. and E.)

Ex. V-6:

1. It's 10:40.
2. It's 1:00.
3. It's 8:10.
4. It's 6:05.
5. It's 9:45.
6. 2:30
7. 7:55
8. 12:20
9. 5:15
10. 3:00

Ex. V-7:

1. It's three o'clock.
2. It's two o'clock.
3. It's eight-ten.
4. It's twelve-o-five.
5. It's four o'clock.
6. It's ten-thirty.
7. It's nine o'clock.
8. It's eleven-forty-five.
9. It's one-twenty.
10. It's seven-thirty-five.

Ex. V-8:

1. 6:15 A.M.
2. in the afternoon
3. in the evening
4. 7:30 P.M.
5. 10 P.M.
6. in the morning
7. It's from 8 in the morning to 4 in the afternoon.

III. Reading

Ex. R-1:

1. Mexico
2. factory
3. Tuesday, Thursday, and Friday
4. 8 A.M. to 5 P.M.
5. home
6. 12:30 . . . 1 P.M.
7. breaks
8. 6 o'clock
9. 2
10. very tired

IV. Structure

Ex. S-1:

1. cities
2. countries
3. glasses
4. families
5. children
6. bosses
7. classes
8. women
9. matches
10. brushes
11. men
12. secretaries
13. universities
14. lives

Ex. S-3:

1. Are aren't
2. Is isn't
3. Is isn't
4. Are aren't
5. Is isn't
6. Are 'm not
7. Am aren't
8. Are 'm not
9. Is he isn't
10. Are they aren't

Ex. S-4:

1. What
2. Who
3. When
4. What
5. Who
6. When
7. What
8. What day

V. Writing

Who are those people?
They are factory workers.
Work is from 8 A.M. to 4 P.M.
Lunch is at noon.
They are tired at 5 o'clock.
Dinner is at 7 o'clock.

Who are those people? They are factory workers. Work is from 8 A.M. to 4 P.M. Lunch is at noon. They are tired at 5 o'clock. Dinner is at 7 o'clock.

VIII. Lifeskills

Ex. L-1:

1. It's on Thursday at 1 P.M.
2. It's Wednesday.
3. It's at 3:30 P.M.
4. It is Dr. Pane.
5. Yes, it is.
6. No, it isn't.
7. It's in the afternoon.

Ex. L-2:

1. It's at 7 and 9:30 P.M.
2. It is at 7 P.M.
3. No, it isn't.
4. Yes, it is.
5. Yes, it is.
6. It is at 6 P.M.
7. It is open from 1 to 5 P.M.
8. It is open at 2 o'clock.
9. No, it isn't.

Ex. L-3:

1. It's cloudy.
2. Yes, it is.
3. It's sunny.
4. No, it isn't.
5. It's 50 degrees.
6. It's 50 degrees.
7. It's foggy.
8. No, it isn't.
9. It's 30 degrees.
10. It's sunny.
11. It's 70 degrees.

VIII. Critical Thinking

A.

1. angry/mad
2. worried
3. listening
4. boss
5. talking
6. worker
7. This person is upset.
8. He is angry at the worker.

B.

1. relaxed
2. proud
3. baby stroller
4. happy
5. glad
6. mother
7. This person is pleased.
8. She is proud of her child.

UNIT 3—Money

I. Vocabulary

Ex. V-1:

1. It's twelve-twenty. It's twenty after twelve. It's twenty past twelve.
2. It's eight-ten. It's ten after eight. It's ten past eight.
3. It's four-thirty. It's half-past four.
4. It's seven-fifteen. It's a quarter after seven.
5. It's ten-forty-five. It's a quarter to eleven.

Ex. V-2: (The teacher should have a large calendar that students can refer to.)

31, 30, 28, 29

__________, __________, December, May, September, __________

Ex. V-3:

June sixth, nineteen ninety-one
July fourth, seventeen seventy-six
November twenty-second, nineteen sixty-three

Ex. V-4:

Winter, Fall/Autumn, __________, __________, __________, __________, __________

Ex. V-5: (Teacher dictates cardinal number from H. #1-6: students write numbers; #7 & 8: students write words.)

Ex. V-6:

1. 2, 2
2. 9, 1
3. 4, 4, 1
4. 2, 1, 5
5. Accept any reasonable answer.

Ex. V-7:

1. 5
2. 4
3. 5
4. 10
5. 8

Ex. V-8:

1. They don't have enough money.
2. She has enough money.
3. He has enough money.
4. We don't have enough money.

III. Reading

Ex. R-1:

1. work
2. the end of the month
3. bank account
4. future
5. budget
6. spend
7. house/university education

IV. Structure

Ex. S-1:

1. are
2. is
3. are
4. Is
5. Are
6. is
7. Is
8. are
9. is
10. Is

Ex. S-2:

1. save
2. cash
3. spends
4. buy
5. sells
6. change
7. count
8. give
9. takes
10. needs

Ex. S-3:

1. him
2. her
3. them
4. us
5. it
6. me
7. you

Ex. S-4:

1. They
2. them
3. I
4. us
5. him

Ex. S-5:

1. Which
2. Where
3. How much
4. Where
5. Which
6. How much

V. Writing

Mrs. Benson gets a paycheck on Friday.
She deposits the money in the bank.
She buys groceries.
She pays the rent.
She is on a budget.
She saves for her family.

Mrs. Benson gets a paycheck on Friday. She deposits the money in the bank. She buys groceries. She pays the rent. She is on a budget. She saves for her family.

VII. Lifeskills

Ex. L-1:

1. It's December 21st.
2. It's November 2nd.
3. There are 5.
4. It's Wednesday.
5. It's December 28th.
6. NOV

1	2	3	4	5	6	7
8	9	10	11	12	13	14
15	16	17	18	19	(20)	21

Ex. L-2:

1. $5.00 - 1.09 = $3.91
2. $2.00 + .99 = $2.99
3. She has $1.05. She buys eggs.
4. $29.99 + 1.80 = $31.79

Ex. L-3:

1. $200
2. $550
3. $50
4. $125

Ex. L-4:

1\.

Date: Oct. 7, 1991.

Pay to: Bob's Store $31.79

Thirty-One and 79/100 Dollars

Carl Rodgers

2\.

Date: March 14, 1991.

Pay to: Nancy's Department Store $63.59

Sixty-Three and 59/100 Dollars

Bianca Jagger

VIII. Critical Thinking

A.

1. She looks at the product.
2. The supermarket sells items.
3. She is careful.
4. The woman wears glasses.
5. She thinks about the item.
6. She examines the package.

B.

1. It is an advertisement.
2. The advertisement sells beer.
3. The advertisement is outside.
4. This is a billboard.
5. It is not in English.
6. There is no price.

UNIT 4—Family and Community

III. Reading

Ex. R-1:

1. water department
2. 8:30
3. grandmother
4. in front of
5. a donut and coffee
6. Her aunt
7. at 9:00
8. her husband
9. She has dinner with her mother.
10. No. she doesn't.
11. She likes to live close to her family and work.

IV. Structure

Ex. S-1:

1. don't walk
2. doesn't drive
3. don't see
4. don't know
5. doesn't get

Ex. S-2:

1. Does _____ know
2. Do _____ see
3. Do _____ work
4. Do _____ practice
5. Does _____ copy

Ex. S-3:

1. cleans
2. don't wash
3. Do _____ watch
4. Do _____ speak
5. doesn't write
6. Are
7. studies
8. walks
9. Do _____ talk
10. don't read
11. is
12. listen
13. don't cook
14. Does _____ close
15. watches

Ex. S-4:

1. Mr. Lee's house
2. Maria's job
3. the student's book
4. Canada's flag
5. the restaurant's sign
6. the park's trees
7. the states' parks
8. the recreation centers' programs
9. the libraries' books
10. the countries' problems

Ex. S-5:

1. I like my sister's room.
2. Mr. Pardee buys that store's fruit.
3. Bill works at Mr. Clease's factory.
4. Kevin sells those companies' radios.
5. The teacher reads the students' papers.

Ex. S-6:

1. her
2. his
3. their
4. my
5. our
6. its
7. your

Ex. S-7:

1. his
2. their
3. her
4. its

Ex. S-8:

1. hers
2. his
3. theirs
4. Mine
5. ours

Ex. S-9:

1. our
2. my
3. mine
4. Theirs
5. her/yours
6. their
7. her
8. hers
9. their
10. mine

Ex. S-10:

1. on the corner of
2. across from
3. between
4. in front of
5. in back of
6. in
7. at (in)
8. on
9. on the corner of
10. at
11. in
12. across from
13. next to

Ex. S-11:

1. It's on the corner of King Drive and Whitman Ave., across from the park.
2. It's on the corner of King Drive and Whitman Ave., across from the police station.
3. It's on the corner of King Drive and Thoreau Street.
4. It's on the corner of King Drive and Thoreau Street, in front of the fire station.

V. Writing

Maria wakes up at six o'clock.
She takes a shower.
She gets dressed.
She leaves her house at eight o'clock.
She gets to work at nine.

Maria wakes up at six o'clock. She takes a shower. She gets dressed. She leaves her house at eight o'clock. She gets to work at nine.

Ex. L-1:

1. grandfather
2. husband
3. niece
4. son
5. aunt
6. brother-in-law
7. cousins
8. grandchildren
9. She is 34 years old.
10. He is 77 years old.

Ex. L-3:

1. Second Street/Lincoln Avenue
2. Emerson between First/Second Avenues
3. Tubman Avenue/Fire Station/Park
4. Emerson/Third/Third Street/Lincoln Avenue
5. Lincoln/right/Third/left

Ex. L-4:

1. employment office
2. museum
3. bakery
4. post office
5. bus station
6. Chinese restaurant
7. movie theater
8. laundromat/Third
9. Department of Motor Vehicles
10. bank/Lincoln Avenue/First Street
11. library
12. parking lot/Second/Emerson Avenues
13. legal aid clinic/First
14. day care center
15. Social Security office

VIII. Critical Thinking

A.

1. a crowded freeway
2. many cars
3. traffic problems
4. more pollution
5. slow
6. Few passengers are in each car.
7. A passenger listens to the radio.

B.

1. a train
2. a train station
3. no traffic problem
4. less pollution
5. fast
6. Many passengers are in the train.
7. A passenger can read the newspaper.

UNIT 5—Parts of the Body

III. Reading

Ex. R-1:

1. Gilbert works for a large electronics company. Doug works for a small gas station.
2. Gilbert has medical insurance.
3. His electronics company pays the medical bills.
4. Gilbert goes to a doctor.
5. Doug waits and doesn't go to a doctor.
6. Doug goes to a health clinic only when it is necessary.
7. Doug has no medical insurance because his company doesn't have it.

IV. Structure

Ex. S-1:

1. a
2. an
3. a
4. an

Ex. S-2:

1. a
2. a
3. an
4. a/the
5. a
6. The/the or a

Ex. S-3:

1. some
2. any
3. anything
4. Someone
5. anyone

Ex. S-4:

1. He doesn't have any on his legs.
2. He has some on his face.
3. He has some on his neck.
4. He doesn't have any on his stomach.
5. He doesn't have any on his feet.

Ex. S-5:

1. knows
2. is
3. works
4. is

Ex. S-6:

1. anything
2. anybody
3. anybody
4. anything
5. anyone

Ex. S-7:

1. Because she picks up many big boxes.
2. Because he plays soccer very hard.
3. Because he doesn't have money for the operation.
4. Because she has a new boyfriend.
5. Because he works all night.

Ex. S-8:

1. gets
2. washes
3. doesn't feel
4. Does . . . take
5. hurts
6. doesn't have
7. Do . . . make
8. exercise
9. are
10. goes
11. studies
12. don't get

V. Writing

Why is Mary tired?
She works in a hospital.
She is a nurse.
She works from 9 P.M. to 6 A.M.
She helps many people.
She is always busy at work.
She doesn't sleep all night.

Why is Mary tired? She works in a hospital. She is a nurse. She works from 9 P.M. to 6 A.M. She helps many people. She is always busy at work. She doesn't sleep all night.

VII. Lifeskills

Ex. L-1:

1. Anthony, Don, and Rosemary have a fever.
2. Linda has a normal temperature.
3. Don's temperature is 103°.
4. Rosemary's temperature is a little over 100°.
5. Linda's temperature is 98.6°.
6. Anthony's temperature is almost 102°.

Ex. L-2:

1. stomachache
2. sore feet
3. sore throat
4. headache
5. backache
6. broken leg

Ex. L-3:

Dear Mrs. Smith:

Please excuse my son Ted from school today. He has an earache. Thank you very much.

Sincerely,

____

VIII. Critical Thinking

A.	B.
1. woman	1. man
2. face	2. body
3. makeup	3. exercise
4. She is at home.	4. He is at a health club.
5. She puts on makeup.	5. He exercises.

UNIT 6—Health

III. Reading

1. He is watching TV.
2. It's a medical story.
3. He has a heart problem.
4. Because he is curious.
5. He doesn't keep the medicine out of reach of children.
6. He takes him to the emergency room at the hospital.

IV. Structure

Ex. S-1:

1. is talking
2. are watching
3. is making
4. are swimming
5. are crying
6. is helping

Ex. S-2:

1. am not coming
2. aren't coughing
3. isn't planning
4. aren't taking
5. aren't going
6. isn't writing

Ex. S-3:

1. Is . . . working
2. Is . . . trying
3. Are . . . waiting
4. Are . . . leaving
5. Are . . . running
6. Is . . . going

Ex. S-4:

1. is calling
2. are making
3. Are . . . checking
4. isn't coming
5. is reading
6. Is . . . planning
7. is sending
8. are keeping
9. isn't working
10. is examining

Ex. S-5:

1. strong medicine
2. big box
3. nurse . . . nice
4. bad cough
5. sore throat
6. hospital . . . expensive
7. correct dosage

Ex. S-6:

1. in
2. on
3. in
4. under
5. on
6. in
7. under
8. on
9. under
10. on . . . in

V. Writing

Mrs. White is feeling healthy.
She eats good food.
She likes fruits and vegetables.
She gets lots of rest.
She doesn't worry too much.
She exercises every day.
She takes a long walk.

Mrs. White is feeling healthy. She eats good food. She likes fruits and vegetables. She gets lots of rest. She doesn't worry too much. She exercises every day. She takes a long walk.

VII. Life Skills

Ex. L-1:

1. Cardiologist
2. Pediatrician
3. Orthopedist
4. Surgeon
5. Psychiatrist
6. General Practitioner
7. Radiologist
8. Allergist
9. Obstetrician

Ex. L-2:

1a. 3
b. 21
2a. The eye needs this medicine.
b. "As desired" He uses the medicine when he wants.
3a. 8 (if needed)
b. 8
c. You shake it well.
4a. Leslie Evans
b. Dr. Pile
c. One capsule 4 times a day for 7 days
d. Penicillin
e. No, it expires in January of 1993.
f. No, it isn't.

VIII. Critical Thinking

A.

1. inside
2. cigarettes
3. emphysema
4. They are talking.
5. They are smoking.
6. They are in a cafe.

B.

1. outside
2. alcohol
3. alcoholism
4. He is alone.
5. He is drinking alcohol.
6. He is on the sidewalk.

7. This is an unhealthy thing to do.

UNIT 7—Food

III. Reading

Ex. R.1:

1. He has a big breakfast, usually with bacon or sausage and eggs.
2. No, he doesn't.
3. He eats a lot of snacks between meals.
4. He eats a couple of candy bars in the afternoon.
5. He drinks sodas all day.
6. He likes fast food restaurants.

(continued)

7. He has frozen dinners.
8. He is telling him that he is overweight and his cholesterol is very high.
9. He eats high cholesterol food, snacks, sodas, frozen dinners, and junk food.
   He doesn't eat fruits and vegetables.
   He doesn't have a balanced diet.

IV. Structure

Ex. S-1:

1. smaller
2. busier
3. more nutritious
4. higher
5. tastier
6. more difficult
7. riper
8. easier
9. sweeter
10. optional answer

Ex. S-2:

1. most difficult
2. ripest
3. smallest
4. softest
5. busiest
6. longest
7. most nutritious
8. saltiest
9. oldest
10. optional answer/more expensive

Ex. S-3:

1. better
2. worse
3. best
4. worst
5. optional answer/best

Ex. S-4:

1. some
2. a
3. a
4. some
5. some
6. a
7. some

Ex. S-5:

1. many
2. much
3. much
4. many
5. much
6. many
7. much
8. many
9. much
10. much

Ex. S-6:

1. few
2. a little
3. a few
4. little
5. a few
6. little
7. few
8. a little
9. little
10. little

Ex. S-7:

1. can
2. can
3. can

V. Writing

Patricia has a small breakfast.
She eats a sandwich for lunch.
She drinks two glasses of milk every day.
She prepares a well-balanced meal every evening.
She goes to a restaurant once a month.
She doesn't like junk food.

Patricia has a small breakfast. She eats a sandwich for lunch. She drinks two glasses of milk every day. She prepares a well-balanced meal every evening. She goes to a restaurant once a month. She doesn't like junk food.

VII. Life Skills

Ex. L-1:

1. Beth's grocery store has the cheaper steak.
   It is a boneless New York strip steak at Best Supermarket and a T-Bone steak at Beth's.
2. Beth's has the cheaper tomatoes.
3. Best's has the more expensive yogurt.
4. The safflower oil is more expensive than the corn oil.
5. $3.99 + 2 ($ .69) = $5.37
   $3.00 + 2.00 = $5.00
   Mr. Suds has the cheaper bill.

Ex. L-2:

Essential	Not Essential Food
fruit	potato chips
vegetables	cola
water	candy
grains	cookies
bread	doughnuts

Ex. L-3:

1. The name is basic lentil soup.
2. brown rice
3. You use two small garlic buds.
4. You use two medium carrots.
5. You need one medium onion.
6. You use a pinch of salt.
7. It serves six people.

Ex. L-4:

1. It costs $4.35.
2. It comes with bread and butter.
3. Spaghetti with no meatballs is more expensive.
4. There are four.
5. They are the same price.
6. Today's special is liver and onions.
7. clam chowder $1.75
   hamburger 3.95
   apple pie 2.00
   milk .55

   Total $8.25

   No, he doesn't need any more money.

VIII. Critical Thinking

A.	B.
1. plates	
2. knife and fork	
3. beginning of a meal	3. end of a meal
4. He's ready to eat.	4. He doesn't want anymore.
5. He is starting his dinner.	5. He is finishing his dinner.
6. cup	6. glass
7. Boy, he's hungry!	7. So much wasted food!

UNIT 8—Clothing

III. Reading

Ex. R-1:

1. He is a compulsive buyer.
2. Betty walked by herself to the mall.
3. She wanted to buy some shoes and a new dress.
4. She stopped in a store called The Fashion Place.
5. She tried on a white and blue dress.
6. It fit very nicely.
7. She didn't buy any shoes because she was very tired.
8. There was a hole in the dress.
9. She returned to the store and exchanged it for another one.

IV. Structure

Ex. S-1:

1. study . . . are studying
2. rents . . . is renting
3. wears . . . is wearing
4. buy . . . are buying
5. wash . . . are washing

Ex. S-2:

1. am sewing . . . sew
2. is wearing white shoes . . . wears
3. are studying so hard . . . study
4. am walking to school . . . walk

Ex. S-3:

1. ourselves
2. myself
3. himself
4. themselves
5. herself
6. yourself
7. itself

Ex. S-4:

1. were
2. was
3. Were
4. wasn't
5. was
6. were
7. were
8. Was
9. was
10. wasn't

Ex. S-5:

1. sewed
2. tied
3. washed
4. buttoned
5. zipped
6. fixed

Ex. S-6:

1. didn't clean
2. didn't turn
3. didn't exchange
4. didn't receive
5. didn't look

Ex. S-7:

1. Did . . . like
2. Did . . . iron
3. Did . . . wash
4. Did . . . rinse
5. Did . . . tie

Ex. S-8:

1. wanted
2. Did . . . attend
3. didn't use
4. Did . . . clean
5. planned
6. didn't ask
7. did . . . open
8. didn't need
9. exchanged
10. purchased

V. Writing

Mr. Moody walked by himself to the department store last Tuesday.
He looked at men's clothes.
He tried on a pair of grey pants.
They fit very well.
They were on sale.
He paid for them with cash.
He returned home by himself.

Mr. Moody walked by himself to the department store last Tuesday. He looked at men's clothes. He tried on a pair of grey pants. They fit very well. They were on sale. He paid for them with cash. He returned home by himself.

VI. Pronunciation

(Teacher will dictate regular and irregular past tense verbs.)

VII. Life Skills

Ex. L-1:

1. a
2. b
3. c
4. b
5. a
6. b

Ex. L-2:

1. No
2. Yes
3. No
4. No
5. Yes
6. No
7. Yes
8. Yes

Ex. L-3:

1. It is made of polyester and cotton.
2. One pair of socks costs $3.25.
3. A pair of tennis shoes costs $37.99.
4. They are white, black, red or yellow.
   They are made of leather.
5. One knit shirt costs $8.50.
6. They are white or black.
7. No, she can't. The largest size is 9.
8. No, the sale ends on May 8th.
9. You can choose from 12 colors.
10. Optional

VIII. Critical Thinking

A.	B.
1. recycling clothing	
2. donation truck	2. clothing racks
3. She doesn't need	3. He needs.
4. She can afford new clothes.	4. He can't afford new clothes.
5. She gives clothing to a second hand store.	5. He is shopping at a second hand store.
6. She cleaned out her closet.	6. He walked to the store.

UNIT 9—Housing

III. Reading

Ex. R-1:

1. He lived in a quiet place in the country.
2. He moved to the city.
3. It seemed crowded and there are many homeless people on the street.
4. He looked for an apartment in the newspaper.
5. The rents were very high.
6. He called an old friend, Kevin.
7. Kevin's brother needed a roommate.
8. He shared the apartment and rent with his new roommate, James.

IV. Structure

Ex. S-1:

1. read
2. found
3. drove
4. got
5. began

Ex. S-2:

1. didn't set
2. didn't sleep
3. didn't catch
4. didn't feel
5. didn't cut

Ex. S-3:

1. Did . . . spend
2. Did . . . meet
3. Did . . . feed
4. Did . . . see
5. Did . . . freeze

Ex. S-4:

1. Did . . . sweep
2. spread
3. lost
4. didn't keep
5. built
6. Did . . . give
7. didn't grow
8. woke
9. Did . . . make
10. didn't hear

Ex. S-5:

1. of
2. for
3. with
4. for
5. with
6. of
7. for
8. for
9. of
10. with

Ex. S-6:

1. should
2. should
3. should
4. should
5. should

V. Writing

Mrs. Sun looked for an apartment.
She found one in the newspaper.
She likes it.
The kitchen is big and modern.
The living room has a view.
There isn't any garage.
It is in a good location.
The neighborhood is quiet.

Mrs. Sun looked for an apartment. She found one in the newspaper. She likes it. The kitchen is big and modern. The living room has a view. There isn't any garage. It is in a good location. The neighborhood is quiet.

VII. Life Skills

Ex. L-1:

1. furnished
2. 555-4573
3. San Carlos
4. The unfurnished apartment in Daly City is cheaper.
5. No, some are more expensive.
6. George Bell at 555-0987
7. The unfurnished house in Belmont has a fireplace.
8. Yes, it has a laundry room.
9. 555-7986
10. It's close to transportation and has carpets.

Ex. L-2:

1. It costs $64.88.
2. 21
3. You have to assemble it.
4. You put it in the living room.
5. You keep it in the closet.
6. It was $44.99.

VIII. Critical Thinking

1. shelter
2. home

A.	B.
4. nest	4. apartment
5. bird	5. family
6. The bird got materials and made a nest.	6. They found an apartment and moved in.
7. The bird has 3 eggs.	7. The family is standing near the apartment.

UNIT 10—Jobs

III. Reading

Ex. R-1:

1. She worked as a hotel clerk.
2. Yes, she did.
3. She needed to learn English.
4. One of her classmates told her about the job.
5. It was an assembly job.
6. It was minimum wage with no benefits, boring, and there were chemical smells.

IV. Structure

Ex. S-1:

1. cut
2. Did . . . repair
3. took
4. didn't file
5. drove
6. Did . . . mow
7. didn't clean
8. used
9. didn't stock
10. got

Ex. S-2:

1. will take
2. will make
3. will fix
4. will talk
5. will paint

Ex. S-3:

1. won't work
2. won't give
3. won't go
4. won't apply
5. won't check

Ex. S-4:

1. Will . . . fill
2. Will . . . see
3. Will . . . change
4. Will . . . deliver
5. Will . . . report

Ex. S-5:

1. will talk
2. won't earn
3. Will . . . take
4. will deliver
5. Will . . . write
6. will call
7. won't be
8. will work
9. Will . . . get
10. won't ask

Ex. S-6:

1. is too.
2. my cousin is too.
3. The package arrived and the letter did too.
4. The carpenter came and the plumber did too.
5. Martin will leave early and Jack will too.
6. You will stay there and my sister will too.
7. Sam works at a restaurant and Max does too.
8. The TV was broken and the radio was too.

V. Writing

Kim works at an office.
She is a secretary.
She types letters and takes shorthand.
Her boss is very nice.
Kim works from 8 A.M. to 4 P.M.
Her salary is $2000 a month.
She has benefits.

Kim works at an office. She is a secretary. She types letters and takes shorthand. Her boss is very nice. Kim works from 8 A.M. to 4 P.M. Her salary is $2000 a month. She has benefits.

VII. Life Skills

Ex. L-1:

1. cashier
2. cook and cashier
3. cashier . . . management
4. apartment manager
5. Rich at 555-9916
6. phones
7. cashier
8. older
9. dental receptionist
10. 12 units

Ex. L-2:

1. manager
2. motel clerk
3. assembler
4. secretary

VIII. Critical Thinking

1. outside
2. signs
3. not happy

A.

4. They are holding signs.
5. They worked there before.
6. These workers are on strike.
7. They don't like their working conditions.

B.

4. He is holding a sign for a job.
5. This person is asking for work.
6. He is unemployed.
7. He needs a job.

UNIT 11—Transportation

III. Reading

Ex. R-1:

1. It took her 45 minutes.
2. She decided to buy a car.
3. They were too expensive.
4. She found it in the want-ads.
5. Yes, they were.
6. Yes, it did.
7. She called a mechanic.
8. Her car needed a lot of repair.
9. She decided to sell the car and take the bus.
10. Optional
11. Optional

IV. Structure

Ex. S-1:

1. is going to give
2. is going to need
3. are going to put
4. is going to stop
5. are going to buy

Ex. S-2:

1. aren't going to cross
2. isn't going to stay
3. aren't going to change
4. am not going to read
5. isn't going to drive

Ex. S-3:

1. Are . . . going to walk
2. Is . . . going to tell
3. Is . . . going to stop
4. Is . . . going to ask
5. Are . . . going to check

Ex. S-4:

1. Are . . . going to drive
2. 'm going to take
3. isn't going to get
4. are going to pay
5. Is . . . going to go
6. isn't going to wash
7. are going to pick
8. Are . . . going to check
9. isn't going to land
10. is going to park

Ex. S-5:

1. must
2. must
3. must
4. have to
5. has to
6. have to

Ex. S-6:

1. has to/must
2. have to/must
3. has to/must

Ex. S-7:

1. Exit
2. Don't write
3. Close
4. Don't go
5. Don't take/Take
6. come

Ex. S-8:

1. Let's call
2. Let's check
3. Let's not sit
4. Let's do

Ex. S-9:

1. Frank isn't either.
2. We aren't talking and the bus driver isn't either.
3. The cable car doesn't go downtown and the train doesn't either.
4. The boat didn't leave and the yacht didn't either.
5. I won't drive over the speed limit and he won't either.
6. Val isn't going to take a vacation and Gilbert isn't either.

V. Writing

Luis takes the bus to school.
He waits at the bus stop at 8:00.
The bus comes at 8:10.
It is always crowded.
He meets his friend on the bus.
They get off the bus at 8:40.
They arrive at school at 8:50.
School starts at 9:00.

Luis takes the bus to school. He waits at the bus stop at 8:00. The bus comes at 8:10. It is always crowded. He meets his friend on the bus. They get off the bus at 8:40. They arrive at school at 8:50. School starts at 9:00.

VII. Life Skills

Ex. L-1:

1. d
2. f
3. b
4. h
5. a
6. e
7. g
8. c

Ex. L-2:

1. c
2. c
3. a
4. b

Ex. L-3

1. 6:30 A.M.
2. 2 hours
3. 6 A.M./$15
4. 1:30 P.M.

Ex. L-4:

1. 57
2. Oak Street
3. Main Street
4. Yes, it does.
5. Every 15 minutes
6. No, he can't.

VIII. Critical Thinking

1. commuters
2. transportation
3. They are going somewhere.

A.

4. freeway
5. car pollution
6. The freeway is crowded.
7. The cars are moving slowly.

B.

4. train station
5. public transportation
6. The train is stopping for passengers.
7. They are getting on and off the train.

UNIT 12—Communication

III. Reading

Ex. R-1:

1. He wasn't home.
2. She had free tickets and wanted to invite him to a musical.
3. He got it on his answering machine.
4. The theme was world peace.
5. She was proud of her brother because he was a good singer.
6. He was a singer.
7. Yes, he did.
8. They planned to pick him up at 7:30.

IV. Structure

Ex. S-1:

Karen is planning now for her trip to the city tomorrow. She will visit the art and history museums. She loves paintings and history. Her mother is a painter and her uncle teaches world history at the local college.

Last week she went to the zoo with her friends. They had a great time. The weather was nice and the animals were very interesting. She took a lot of pictures.

	Verb	Tense
1.	is planning	present continuous
2.	will visit	future
3.	loves	present
4.	is	present
5.	teaches	present
6.	went	past
7.	had	past
8.	was	past
9.	were	past
10.	took	past

Ex. S-2:

1. calls
2. sent
3. will perform/are going to perform
4. am writing
5. Did . . . deliver
6. Do . . . put
7. Will . . . insure/Is . . . going to insure
8. Is . . . dialing
9. Was
10. won't look/aren't going to look
11. didn't forward
12. doesn't answer
13. aren't renting
14. isn't

Ex. S-3:

1. sent
2. will go/are going to go
3. am looking
4. Did . . . find
5. drives
6. didn't leave
7. Will . . . play/Are . . . going to play
8. Do . . . listen
9. will act
10. Is . . . watching
11. won't pay/'m not going to pay
12. don't like
13. Will . . . go/Are . . . going to go
14. were
15. isn't doing

Ex. S-4:

1. should
2. can
3. must/has to
4. should
5. can

Ex. S-5:

1. phones
2. directories
3. passes
4. plays
5. children
6. watches
7. teeth
8. lives
9. women
10. libraries

Ex. S-6:

1. many
2. much
3. much
4. many
5. much

Ex. S-7:

1. little
2. few
3. few
4. little
5. little

Ex. S-8:

1. John's pen
2. Kathy's letters
3. The telephone companies' rates
4. I saw the mail carrier's truck.
5. Mary likes the museums' paintings.

Ex. S-9:

1. me
2. She
3. they
4. us
5. my
6. theirs
7. yourself
8. himself
9. any
10. some

Ex. S-10:

1. new (young)
2. wrong
3. slow
4. clean
5. cold
6. poor
7. thin
8. quiet
9. difficult
10. hard
11. tall
12. open

Ex. S-11:

1. taller
2. busiest
3. more beautiful
4. bigger
5. most difficult
6. best
7. worse

Ex. S-12:

1. on
2. with
3. for
4. in
5. between
6. under
7. on/in
8. At/under

V. Writing

I went to the city last week.
I visited a science museum.
It was very interesting.
I liked the exhibit about astronomy the best.
I want to be an astronaut.
Maybe in the future we will live in space.
See you later.

I went to the city last week. I visited a science museum. It was very interesting. I liked the exhibit about astronomy the best. I want to be an astronaut. Maybe in the future we will live in space. See you later.

VII. Life Skills

Ex. L-1:

1. Club Dr.
2. 555-8695
3. 555-8967
4. 555-3423
5. 21341 Harding St.
6. 555-8734
7. 555-9812

Ex. L-2:

1. You save 60% from 11 P.M. to 8 A.M.
2. Regular rates are week days 8 A.M. to 5 P.M.
3. The cheapest times for Bruce to call his friend on the 4th of July are 11 P.M. to 8 A.M.

Ex. L-3:

1. 2 and 7:30 P.M.
2. It will take place in the Hall of Flowers, Kennedy Park.
3. The Bad Boys
4. It is playing classical music.
5. He can see it at 8 P.M.
6. They can go from June 13th to the 18th, 10 A.M. to 4 P.M.
7. She can go Sunday at 2 P.M.
8. He can go to a free concert at Central Park on Sunday at 1 P.M.

VIII. Critical Thinking

A.

1. outside
2. wall
3. realism
4. mural
5. They are looking at the mural.
6. They are recognizing the pictures in the mural.

B.

1. inside
2. museum
3. abstract
4. a painting
5. She is looking at a painting.
6. She is thinking about the meaning of the painting.